Contents

Contents

Strategy Workshop

As you listen to the story "The Pumpkin Box," by Angela Johnson, you will stop from time to time to do some activities on these practice pages. These activities will help you think about different strategies that can help you read better. After completing each activity, you will discuss what you've written with your classmates and talk about how to use these strategies.

Remember, strategies can help you become a better reader. Good readers

- use strategies whenever they read

- use different strategies before, during, and after reading

- think about how strategies will help them

Strategy 1: Predict/Infer

Use this strategy before and during reading to help make predictions about what happens next or what you're going to learn.

Here's how to use the Predict/Infer Strategy:

1. Think about the title, the illustrations, and what you have read so far.
2. Tell what you think will happen next—or what you will learn. Thinking about what you already know on the topic may help.
3. Try to figure out things the author does not say directly.

Listen as your teacher begins "The Pumpkin Box." When your teacher stops, complete the activity to show that you understand how to predict what the pumpkin box is.

Think about the story and respond to the question below.

What do you think the pumpkin box is?

_____

_____

_____

_____

As you continue listening to the story, think about whether your prediction was right. You might want to change your prediction or write a new one below.

_____

_____

_____

_____

_____

Name _____

Strategy 2: Phonics/Decoding

Use this strategy during reading when you come across a word you don't know.

Here's how to use the Phonics/Decoding Strategy:

1. Look carefully at the word.
2. Look for word parts you know and think about the sounds for the letters.
3. Blend the sounds to read the words.
4. Ask yourself: Is this a word I know? Does it make sense in what I am reading?
5. If not, ask yourself: What else can I try? Should I look in a dictionary?

Listen as your teacher continues the story. When your teacher stops, use the Phonics/Decoding Strategy.

Now write down the steps you used to decode the word *munching*.

_____

_____

_____

_____

_____

_____

_____

_____

_____

_____

_____

Remember to use this strategy whenever you are reading and come across a word that you don't know.

Name _____

Strategy 3: Monitor/Clarify

Use this strategy during reading whenever you're confused about what you are reading.

Here's how to use the Monitor/Clarify Strategy:
- Ask yourself if what you're reading makes sense—or if you are learning what you need to learn.
- If you don't understand something, reread, use the illustrations, or read ahead to see if that helps.

Listen as your teacher continues the story. When your teacher stops, complete the activity to show that you understand how to figure out how the pumpkin box got underground.

Think about the pumpkin box and respond below.

1. Describe the pumpkin box.

_____
_____
_____

2. Can you tell from listening to the story how the pumpkin box got there? Why or why not?

_____
_____
_____
_____

3. How can you find out why the pumpkin box was buried in the ground?

_____
_____
_____
_____

Name _____

Strategy 4: Question

Use this strategy during and after reading to ask questions about important ideas in the story.

Here's how to use the Question Strategy:

- Ask yourself questions about important ideas in the story.
- Ask yourself if you can answer these questions.
- If you can't answer the questions, reread and look for answers in the text. Thinking about what you already know and what you've read in the story may help you.

Listen as your teacher continues the story. Then complete the activity to show that you understand how to ask yourself questions about important ideas in the story.

Think about the story and respond below.

Write a question you might ask yourself at this point in the story.

_____

_____

_____

_____

_____

_____

_____

_____

_____

_____

If you can't answer your question now, think about it while you listen to the rest of the story.

Name _____

Strategy 5: Evaluate

Use this strategy during and after reading to help you form an opinion about what you read.

Here's how to use the Evaluate Strategy:

- Tell whether or not you think this story is entertaining and why.
- Is the writing clear and easy to understand?
- This is a realistic fiction story. Did the author make the characters believable and interesting?

Listen as your teacher continues the story. When your teacher stops, complete the activity to show that you are thinking of how you feel about what you are reading and why you feel that way.

Think about the story and respond below.

1. Tell whether or not you think this story is entertaining and why.

_____

_____

_____

_____

2. Is the writing clear and easy to understand?

_____

_____

_____

_____

3. This is a realistic fiction story. Did the author make the characters interesting and believable?

_____

_____

_____

_____

Name _____

Strategy 6: Summarize

Use this strategy after reading to summarize what you read.

Here's how to use the Summarize Strategy:
- Think about the characters.
- Think about where the story takes place.
- Think about the problem in the story and how the characters solve it.
- Think about what happens in the beginning, middle, and end of the story.

Think about the story you just listened to. Complete the activity to show that you understand how to identify important story parts that will help you summarize the story.

Think about the story and respond to the questions below:

1. Who is the main character?

_____

_____

_____

2. Where does the story take place?

_____

_____

_____

3. What is the problem and how is it resolved?

_____

_____

_____

Now use this information to summarize the story for a partner.

8

Name _____

Nature's Fury

After reading each selection, complete the chart below and on the next page to show what you discovered. Sample answers shown.

	What is the setting or settings for the action or descriptions in the selection?	What dangers do people face in the selection?
Earthquake Terror	Magpie Island, in California **(2.5 Points)**	Jonathan and Abby are stranded on Magpie Island when an earthquake strikes, toppling trees all around them. **(2.5)**
Eye of the Storm	Tucson, Arizona and Tornado Alley (Amarillo, Texas and towns in Texas, Oklahoma and Kansas) **(2.5)**	Warren Faidley faces danger from lightning bolts and spiders while photographing from an underpass. He and Tom Willett face danger from tornadoes forming around them in Tornado Alley. **(2.5)**
Volcanoes	Hawaii, Washington state, Iceland, Guatemala, California, Oregon **(2.5)**	People face danger from the eruption of Mount St. Helens; people on the island of Heimaey, Iceland, face danger from a volcano; people in Hawaii face danger to their houses from quick-moving lava. **(2.5)**

Theme 1: **Nature's Fury**   9

Assessment Tip: Total **10** points per selection and **2** points for the final question

Name _____

Nature's Fury

After reading each selection, complete the chart to show what you discovered. Sample answers shown.

	What warnings or events happen before nature's fury occurs in the selection?	What did you learn about an example of nature's fury in the selection?
Earthquake Terror	Moose, the dog, is nervous, barking and shaking. The air is still and there is a deep rumbling sound. **(2.5)**	Most earthquakes occur along the shores of the Pacific Ocean, many of them on the San Andreas fault. **(2.5)**
Eye of the Storm	Cool, moist air meets hot desert air to cause thunderstorms in Arizona. Cool, dry air collides with warm, moist air to cause tornadoes. **(2.5)**	Tornadoes form from funnel clouds. When a funnel cloud touches the ground, it becomes a tornado. **(2.5)**
Volcanoes	Before volcanoes erupt, magma pushes up through cracks in the earth's crust. Before Mount St. Helens erupted, there were thousands of small earthquakes. **(2.5)**	There are different kinds of volcanoes: shield, strato-volcanoes, cinder cone, and dome volcanoes. **(2.5)**

What advice would you give others about the different kinds of nature's fury featured in this theme?

Student answers should reflect an understanding of the dangers and

settings of the different kinds of nature's fury in the theme. **(2)**

Assessment Tip: Total **10** Points per selection and **2** points for the final question

Name _____

A Scientist's Report

Use the words in the box to complete the scientist's report on the Magpie Island earthquake.

Vocabulary

shuddered

debris

undulating

fault

jolt

Earthquake Report

Magpie Island lies near the San Andreas
fault **(2 points)** _____, so it was susceptible to
the recent earthquake. On a cloudless day, witnesses
reported hearing a sound like thunder and feeling a
jolt **(2)** _____ as the earth started to
shake. Next, the ground below their feet
shuddered **(2)** _____ and heaved. Trees began
to fall with a forceful impact. As the earthquake reached
its peak, the ground began undulating **(2)** _____
in a continuous motion.

After the shaking stopped, people examined the
devastation that the earthquake had caused.
Debris **(2)** _____ lay everywhere. The
upheaval had struck a great blow to the island.

Name _____

Event Map

Record in this Event Map the main story events in the order in which they occurred.

Page 30

At first Moose listens. Then he barks and paces back and forth as if he senses that something is wrong. **(2 points)**

Pages 30–31

After Jonathan puts the leash on Moose, they all slowly start to walk back to the camper. **(2)**

Pages 32–33

Jonathan and Abby hear a strange noise. At first Jonathan thinks it is thunder or hunters. Then suddenly he realizes they are caught in an earthquake. **(2)**

Page 35

Abby screams and falls. As Jonathan lunges forward, he tries to catch Abby. Then he shouts, "Stay where you are, I'm coming." **(2)**

Pages 36–37

Jonathan sees the huge redwood tree sway back and forth. Then he scrambles away from it as it falls. **(2)**

Assessment Tip: Total **10** Points

Name _____

True or False?

Read each sentence. Write T if the sentence is true, or F if the sentence is false. If a sentence is false, correct it to make it true.

1. **F** ____ Jonathan and Abby's parents had left the island to go grocery shopping. **(1 point)**
Their parents had gone to get treatment for their mother's broken ankle.

2. **T** ____ Moose became restless because he could feel the earthquake coming.
(1) _____

3. **T** ____ Jonathan thought the first rumblings of the earthquake were distant thunder.
(1) _____

4. **F** ____ Jonathan knew what to do because he had been in an earthquake before.
He had practiced earthquake drills in school. **(1)**

5. **F** ____ When the giant redwood began to fall, Moose dragged Jonathan to safety.
When the giant redwood began to fall, Jonathan crawled out of the way. **(1)**

6. **F** ____ Jonathan and Abby found shelter in a large ditch.
Jonathan and Abby found shelter under the fallen redwood. **(1)**

7. **F** ____ In a panic, Moose ran off and didn't come back.
Jonathan held Moose under the tree with him and Abby. **(1)**

8. **T** ____ As quickly as it had begun, the earthquake stopped and the woods were silent.
(1) _____

Name _____

Mapping the Sequence

Read this passage. Then complete the activity on page 15.

Rapids Ahead!

Alison scanned the river nervously. She had already endured two sets of violent rapids. Each time, she had grasped the ropes of the raft so hard that her knuckles turned white. Luckily, the guide on her raft was strong and skilled. "Relax, Alison," Anushka had smiled when the trip had begun three hours earlier. "Rafting is a blast, once you get the hang of it."

During the first hour on the river, Anushka had taught Alison how to paddle on one side to make the raft go in the opposite direction. She had instructed Alison on what to do if the raft flipped or if she were tossed out. "Don't fight the current," Anushka had said. "Let it carry you downstream as you swim for the shore."

Six months earlier, when Alison's parents had proposed a whitewater rafting trip down the Snake River, Alison said, "No way." Her brother Zack was thrilled, though, so Alison's parents signed all four of them up for a seven-day run. So far, the trip was as bad as Alison had expected.

"Rapids ahead. Hold on!" Anushka said. Alison's stomach knotted as the raft pitched forward with the current. "Paddle left!" Anushka shouted. As Alison's paddle hit the water, the bow of the raft hit a boulder and shot into the air. Alison shut her eyes as icy water drenched her.

When she opened her eyes, Anushka was gone. In a panic, Alison scanned the rapids. "Anushka!" she screamed. Then she saw her. Anushka was making her way to shore, feet first, letting the current do the work. "It's up to me now," Alison said to herself. She paddled left, then right, steering between the rocks. She was amazed that she could control it. Left. Right. Left again. Now Anushka was on the bank, shouting directions over the roar of the river. Alison managed to nose the raft into an eddy and a moment later, onto the shore.

"Great job, Alison!" Anushka grinned. "You really kept your head out there!" Alison beamed. Maybe this trip would be all right after all.

Name _____

Mapping the Sequence continued

Write each story event from page 14 in the sequence map below. Put the events in order.

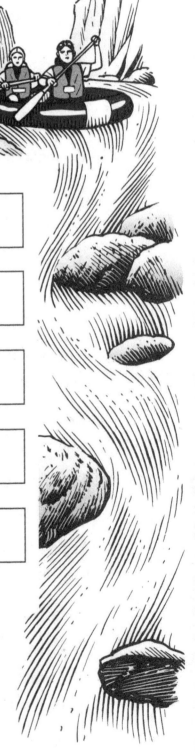

▶ Alison successfully guides the raft to shore.

▶ Anushka tells Alison to relax.

▶ The raft hits a boulder and Anushka falls overboard.

▶ Anushka teaches Alison how to steer the raft.

▶ Alison's parents suggest a raft trip on the Snake River.

Alison's parents suggest a raft trip on the Snake River. **(2 points)**

⬇

Anushka tells Alison to relax. **(2)**

⬇

Anushka teaches Alison how to steer the raft. **(2)**

⬇

The raft hits a boulder and Anushka falls overboard. **(2)**

⬇

Alison successfully guides the raft to shore. **(2)**

Now go back to the passage. Circle the words that helped you understand the following:

▶ when the family plans the trip **(1 point)**

▶ when Anushka tells Alison that rafting is fun **(1)**

▶ when Anushka teaches Alison some basic rafting techniques **(1)**

▶ whether Anushka's spill occurs during the first, second, or third set of rapids that she and Alison encounter **(1)**

Name _____

Getting to Base

Read the sentences. For each underlined word, identify the base word. Write the base word and the ending.

Example: shake + -ing

1. Magpie Island was a popular place for <u>hiking</u>. hike + -ing **(1 point)**

2. Jonathan was nervous about staying in such an <u>isolated</u> place.
   isolate + -ed **(1)**

3. He thought it would be <u>safer</u> to go back to their trailer.
   safe + -er **(1)**

4. Jonathan and Abby followed the trail past blackberry <u>bushes</u>.
   bush + -es **(1)**

5. Neither of them had the <u>slightest</u> idea how the day would end.
   slight + -est **(1)**

6. Moose cocked his head and began <u>sniffing</u> the ground.
   sniff + -ing **(1)**

7. At first the earthquake was a <u>thunderous</u> noise in the distance.
   thunder + -ous **(1)**

8. Trees <u>swayed</u> all around Jonathan and Abby.
   sway + -ed **(1)**

9. The ground began rising and falling like ocean <u>waves</u>.
   wave + -s **(1)**

10. Abby <u>cried</u> for Jonathan to come help her. cry + -ed **(1)**

Assessment Tip: Total **10** Points

Name _____

Short Vowels

Remember that a short vowel sound is usually spelled by one vowel and followed by a consonant sound. This is the **short vowel pattern.** These vowels usually spell short vowel sounds:

/ă/ *a*   /ĕ/ *e*   /ĭ/ *i*   /ŏ/ *o*   /ŭ/ *u*

▶ The short vowel sounds in the starred words do not have the usual short vowel spelling patterns. The /ĕ/ sound is spelled *ea* in *breath* and *deaf.* The /ŭ/ sound is spelled *ou* in *tough* and *rough.*

Write each Spelling Word under its vowel sound.
Order of answers for each category may vary.

/ă/ Sound
staff **(1 point)**

grasp **(1)**

/ĕ/ Sound
slept **(1)**

breath **(1)**

dwell **(1)**

swept **(1)**

deaf **(1)**

/ĭ/ Sound
mist **(1)**

ditch **(1)**

swift **(1)**

split **(1)**

/ŏ/ Sound
dock **(1)**

fond **(1)**

/ŭ/ Sound
bunk **(1)**

bunch **(1)**

stuck **(1)**

tough **(1)**

crush **(1)**

fund **(1)**

rough **(1)**

Spelling Words

1. bunk
2. staff
3. dock
4. slept
5. mist
6. bunch
7. swift
8. stuck
9. breath*
10. tough*
11. fond
12. crush
13. grasp
14. dwell
15. fund
16. ditch
17. split
18. swept
19. deaf*
20. rough*

Name _____

Spelling Spree

Letter Math Add and subtract letters from the words below to make Spelling Words. Write the new words.

1. b + dunk – d = <u>bunk</u> **(1 point)**

2. sl + kept – k = <u>slept</u> **(1)**

3. f + pond – p = <u>fond</u> **(1)**

4. burn – r + ch = <u>bunch</u> **(1)**

5. st + duck – d = <u>stuck</u> **(1)**

6. dw + shell – sh = <u>dwell</u> **(1)**

7. cr + mush – m = <u>crush</u> **(1)**

8. d + rock – r = <u>dock</u> **(1)**

9. m + wrist – wr = <u>mist</u> **(1)**

10. sw + lift – l = <u>swift</u> **(1)**

11. spl + bit – b = <u>split</u> **(1)**

12. t + cough – c = <u>tough</u> **(1)**

13. d + leaf – l = <u>deaf</u> **(1)**

14. gr + clasp – cl = <u>grasp</u> **(1)**

tr

+

Sunk

– s

=

trunk

Phrase Fillers Write the Spelling Word that best completes each phrase.

15. to take a deep <u>breath</u> **(1)**

16. as <u>rough</u> **(1)** as sandpaper

17. to put money into a <u>fund</u> **(1)**

18. to dig a <u>ditch</u> **(1)**

19. <u>swept</u> **(1)** with a broom

20. to join a company's <u>staff</u> **(1)**

18   Theme 1: **Nature's Fury**
Assessment Tip: Total **20** Points

Spelling Words

1. bunk
2. staff
3. dock
4. slept
5. mist
6. bunch
7. swift
8. stuck
9. breath*
10. tough*
11. fond
12. crush
13. grasp
14. dwell
15. fund
16. ditch
17. split
18. swept
19. deaf*
20. rough*

Name _____

Proofreading and Writing

Proofreading Circle the five misspelled Spelling Words in this newspaper article. Then write each word correctly.

Spelling Words

MAGPIE ISLAND — An earthquake struck yesterday, and children are reported to be stranded in the island campground. No one on the campground's (staf) was there at the time. An early report said that "a bunch of kids" were (stouk) on the island. However, it turns out that only two children are there. Rescuers in a boat are reported to be nearing the island's (dok.) A heavy (missed) has slowed the rescue effort. One rescuer said, "It's been (touph) going so far, but we'll get them off the island safely."

Spelling Words

1. bunk
2. staff
3. dock
4. slept
5. mist
6. bunch
7. swift
8. stuck
9. breath*
10. tough*
11. fond
12. crush
13. grasp
14. dwell
15. fund
16. ditch
17. split
18. swept
19. deaf*
20. rough*

1. staff **(1 point)**

2. stuck **(1)**

3. dock **(1)**

4. mist **(1)**

5. tough **(1)**

Write a Description If you were to go to the scene of an earthquake right after it happened, what do you think you would find? What would you see? Whom would you meet?

On a separate piece of paper, write a description of the scene you might encounter. Use Spelling Words from the list. Responses will vary. **(5 points)**

Name _____

Synonym Shakeup

Read the definition of each thesaurus word and its synonyms. Then rewrite the numbered sentences using a different synonym for each underlined word.

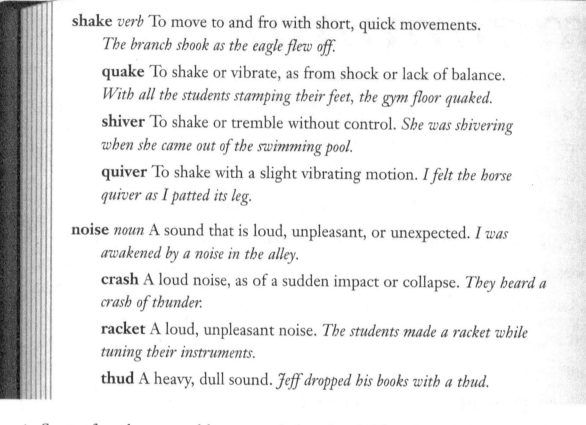

shake *verb* To move to and fro with short, quick movements. *The branch shook as the eagle flew off.*

quake To shake or vibrate, as from shock or lack of balance. *With all the students stamping their feet, the gym floor quaked.*

shiver To shake or tremble without control. *She was shivering when she came out of the swimming pool.*

quiver To shake with a slight vibrating motion. *I felt the horse quiver as I patted its leg.*

noise *noun* A sound that is loud, unpleasant, or unexpected. *I was awakened by a noise in the alley.*

crash A loud noise, as of a sudden impact or collapse. *They heard a crash of thunder.*

racket A loud, unpleasant noise. *The students made a racket while tuning their instruments.*

thud A heavy, dull sound. *Jeff dropped his books with a thud.*

1. Soon after the ground began to <u>shake</u>, the children heard the <u>noise</u> of a deer leaping from the bushes.

   Soon after the ground began to quake, the children heard the crash of

   a deer leaping from the bushes. **(4 points)**

2. Jonathan began to <u>shake</u> from cold and fear, listening to the <u>noise</u> of the crows.

   Jonathan began to shiver from cold and fear, listening to the racket of

   the crows. **(4)**

3. Abby's lip began to <u>shake</u> as she heard the <u>noise</u> of running footsteps.

   Abby's lip began to quiver as she heard the thud of running footsteps. **(4)**

Assessment Tip: Total **12** Points

Name _____

Sensing Danger

Kinds of Sentences There are four kinds of sentences:

1. A declarative sentence tells something and ends with a period.
   Earthquakes occur along fault lines in the earth.

2. An interrogative sentence asks a question and ends with a question mark.
   Can earthquakes be predicted?

3. An imperative sentence gives a request or an order and usually ends with a period.
   Protect your head in an earthquake.

4. An exclamatory sentence expresses strong feeling and ends with an exclamation mark.
   How frightening an earthquake is!

Add the correct punctuation mark to each sentence below.
Then write what kind of sentence each one is.

1. Why is the dog barking? **(1 point)**
   interrogative sentence **(1)**

2. Put him on his leash. **(1)**
   imperative sentence **(1)**

3. Some animals can sense a coming earthquake. **(1)**
   declarative sentence **(1)**

4. How frightened I am! **(1)**
   exclamatory sentence **(1)**

5. The earth has stopped shaking at last. **(1)**
   declarative sentence **(1)**

Assessment Tip: Total **10** Points

Name _____

On Vacation

Subjects and Predicates Every sentence has a subject. It tells whom or what the sentence is about. The complete subject includes all the words in the subject, and the simple subject is the main word or words in the complete subject.

Every sentence has a predicate too. It tells what the subject is or does. The complete predicate includes all the words in the predicate, and the simple predicate is the main word or words in the complete predicate.

Draw a slash mark (/) between the complete subject and the complete predicate in the sentences below. Then circle the simple subject and underline the simple predicate. (3 points each sentence)

1. The whole (family)/travels in our new camper.
2. (Everybody)/helps to pitch the tent under a tree.
3. (They)/will use a compass on their hike.
4. A good (fire)/is difficult to build.
5. The (smell) of cooking/is delicious to the hungry campers.

Assessment Tip: Total **15** Points

Name _____

Sentence Combining

A **compound subject** is made up of two or more simple subjects that have the same predicate. Use a connecting word such as *and* or *or* to join the simple subjects.

Jonathan yelled. **Abby** yelled.   **Jonathan and Abby** yelled.

Combine two simple subjects into one compound subject, as shown above, to make your writing clearer and less choppy.

A **compound predicate** is made up of two or more simple predicates that have the same subject. Use a connecting word such as *and* or *or* to join the simple predicates.

Moose **barked**. Moose **howled**.   Moose **barked and howled**.

Combine simple predicates into compound predicates, as shown above, to make your writing smoother.

Suppose Jonathan wrote a draft of a letter to his aunt about his vacation. Revise his letter by combining sentences. Each new sentence will have either a compound subject or a compound predicate. Only Jonathan's first sentence will remain the same.

What an exciting vacation we had! Mom broke her ankle. Mom had to go to the hospital. Abby stayed on the island. I stayed on the island during an earthquake. Moose barked. Moose warned us. The ground shook. The ground rolled. Have you ever been in an earthquake? Has Uncle Adam ever been in an earthquake?

What an exciting vacation we had! Mom broke her ankle and had

to go to the hospital. Abby and I stayed on the island during an

earthquake. Moose barked and warned us. The ground shook and

rolled. Have you or Uncle Adam ever been in an

earthquake? (**2 points** for each combined sentence)

Name _____

Writing a News Article

Jonathan and Abby Palmer experience firsthand an unforgettable event — the terror of an earthquake. Imagine you are a reporter for the *Daily Gazette*. Use the chart below to gather details for a news article about an interesting or unusual event at your school, in your neighborhood, or in your town. Answer these questions: What happened? Who was involved? When, where, and why did this event occur? How did it happen?

Who? (2 points)
What? (2)
When? (2)
Where? (2)
Why? (2)
How? (2)

Now use the details you gathered to write your news article on a separate sheet of paper. Include a headline and a beginning that will capture your reader's attention. Present facts in order of importance, from most to least important. Try to use quotations from eyewitnesses to bring this news event to life. (3)

24   Theme 1: **Nature's Fury**
Assessment Tip: Total **15** Points

Name _____

Adding Details

A good reporter uses details to explain what happened
and to bring an event to life. Read the following news
article that might have been written about the earthquake.
Then rewrite it on the lines below, adding details from the
list to improve the article.

(**1 point** per detail)

Details

twelve-year-old

in the woods

giant redwood

one-hundred-year-old

for several weeks

under a fallen redwood

afternoon

to the mainland

on Magpie Island

his six-year-old sister

Quake Rocks Campground

A powerful earthquake rocked an isolated
campground in California yesterday. No serious injuries
were reported. Some trees were uprooted, and a bridge
was destroyed. Two members of the Palmer family,
Jonathan and his sister Abby, were trapped during the
quake.

"I was very scared," said Jonathan Palmer. "I'm just
glad no one got hurt. My sister only had a minor cut."

The campground will be closed to visitors until the
debris is cleared and the bridge is repaired.

A powerful earthquake rocked an isolated campground **on Magpie Island** in

California yesterday **afternoon**. No serious injuries were reported. Some

one-hundred-year-old giant redwood trees were uprooted, and a bridge **to the**

mainland was destroyed. Two members of the Palmer family, **twelve-year-old**

Jonathan and his **six-year-old sister** Abby, were trapped **in the woods under a**

fallen redwood during the quake.

"I was very scared," said Jonathan Palmer. "I'm just glad no one got hurt. My

sister only had a minor cut."

The campground will be closed to visitors **for several weeks** until the debris

is cleared and the bridge is repaired.

Name _____

Revising Your Description

Reread your description. Put a checkmark in the box for each sentence that describes your paper. Use this page to help you revise.

Rings the Bell

☐ The beginning tells my topic. The ending is satisfying.

☐ Sensory words and exact details create vivid pictures.

☐ My details are well organized and related to my topic.

☐ Voice is strong; you can tell how I feel about my topic.

☐ Sentences flow smoothly. There are almost no mistakes.

Getting Stronger

☐ The beginning and ending may be somewhat weak.

☐ More exact words and sensory details are needed.

☐ My details could be easier to follow. A few are unrelated.

☐ My voice doesn't come through clearly.

☐ Some sentences are awkward. There are a few mistakes.

Try Harder

☐ The beginning and ending are missing.

☐ There are no details. My word choices are confusing.

☐ The order is unclear. Many details are unrelated.

☐ My writing sounds flat. You can't tell how I feel.

☐ Most sentences are choppy. There are lots of mistakes.

Writing Complete Sentences

**Make each incomplete sentence complete. Change words or add
extra words if you need to.** Answers will vary. Sample answers given.

1. Being a photographer
   Being a photographer can be exciting. **(1 point)**

2. Photographing nature
   Photographing nature can be dangerous. **(1)**

3. Lightning flashing in the sky
   You can take pictures of lightning flashing in the sky. **(1)**

4. Chasing storms
   You could travel the world while chasing storms. **(1)**

5. Tornadoes in the distance
   You could take pictures of tornadoes in the distance. **(1)**

6. The black funnel is impressive, even far away.
   Complete. **(1)**

7. Planes in storms
   Planes can get tossed about in storms. **(1)**

8. A bumpy ride
   Turbulence can create a bumpy ride for passengers. **(1)**

9. Dangerous to be out in some storms
   It's dangerous to be out in some storms. **(1)**

10. Don't stand under a tree when there's lightning.
    Complete. **(1)**

Name _____

Spelling Words

Words Often Misspelled Look for familiar spelling patterns to help you remember how to spell the Spelling Words on this page. Think carefully about the parts that you find hard to spell in each word.

Write the missing letters and apostrophes in the Spelling Words below.

1. en o u g h **(1 point)**
2. c a u g h t **(1)**
3. br o u g h t **(1)**
4. th o u g h t **(1)**
5. ev e ry **(1)**
6. nin e ty **(1)**
7. th e i r **(1)**
8. th e y ' re **(1)**
9. th e r e **(1)**
10. th e r e ' s **(1)**
11. k n ow **(1)**
12. k n ew **(1)**
13. o ' c lock **(1)**
14. w e ' r e **(1)**
15. p e o ple **(1)**

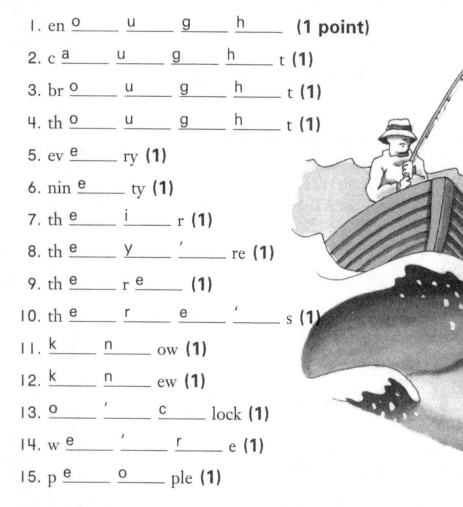

Spelling Words

1. enough
2. caught
3. brought
4. thought
5. every
6. ninety
7. their
8. they're
9. there
10. there's
11. know
12. knew
13. o'clock
14. we're
15. people

Study List On a separate piece of paper, write each Spelling Word. Check your spelling against the words on the list.

Order of words may vary.

Assessment Tip: Total **15** Points

Name _____

Spelling Spree

Word Clues Write the Spelling Word that best fits each clue.

1. the sum of eighty-nine and one
2. a contraction for describing what other people are doing
3. to be aware of a fact
4. a time-telling word
5. as much as is needed
6. a word for other people's belongings
7. took along
8. a contraction for "there is"

1. ninety **(1 point)**
2. they're **(1)**
3. know **(1)**
4. o'clock **(1)**
5. enough **(1)**
6. their **(1)**
7. brought **(1)**
8. there's **(1)**

Spelling Words
1. enough
2. caught
3. brought
4. thought
5. every
6. ninety
7. their
8. they're
9. there
10. there's
11. know
12. knew
13. o'clock
14. we're
15. people

Word Addition Write a Spelling Word by adding the beginning of the first word to the end of the second word.

9. caution + fight
10. we'll + more
11. knight + flew
12. peony + steeple
13. even + wary
14. them + cure
15. think + bought

9. caught **(1)**
10. we're **(1)**
11. knew **(1)**
12. people **(1)**
13. every **(1)**
14. there **(1)**
15. thought **(1)**

Assessment Tip: Total **15** Points

Proofreading and Writing

Proofreading Circle the five misspelled Spelling Words in this announcement. Then write each word correctly.

Spelling Words

1. enough
2. caught
3. brought
4. thought
5. every
6. ninety
7. their
8. they're
9. there
10. there's
11. know
12. knew
13. o'clock
14. we're
15. people

The staff of the Science Museum is pleased to announce that our new Natural Disasters Hall will open to the public next Monday at nine (oclock) in the morning. We've put a lot of (thaught) into this exhibit, and we're sure that you'll enjoy it. Just about (evry) form of nature's fury is represented, from lightning to earthquakes to volcanoes. Even if you already (kno) a lot about the topic, we think you'll learn something new. We hope to see you (their.)

1. o'clock **(1 point)**

2. thought **(1)**

3. every **(1)**

4. know **(1)**

5. there **(1)**

▬▬▬ - **Write Song Titles** Pick five Spelling Words from the list. Then, for each one, make up a song title that includes the word and mentions some form of Nature's Fury. Responses will vary. **(5 points)**

Assessment Tip: Total **10** Points

Name _____

Stormy Weather

Use words from the box to complete the diary entry below.

sizzling
collide
funnel clouds
tornadoes
lightning
rotate
jagged
prairie
severe

May 10, 2000
Dear Diary,

Today was by far the scariest day of my trip. Everything was fine as I crossed the border into Oklahoma. The highway stretched out over a __prairie **(1 point)**__ that seemed to go on forever. As I looked into my rear-view mirror, I spotted some dense clouds forming behind me. "I hope they aren't __funnel clouds **(1)**__," I thought. Then I spotted a flash of __lightning **(1)**__. The clouds started to __rotate **(1)**__, slowly at first, and then faster and faster. A couple of __tornadoes **(1)**__ were forming right before my eyes! I realized that a __severe **(1)**__ storm had formed behind me, and it was moving fast in my direction. The __jagged **(1)**__ bolts of lightning were getting closer. One of the tornadoes lifted a tractor into the air, spun it around, and dropped it. I watched it __collide **(1)**__ with a shed on the ground. Lightning struck a dry bush behind me. It turned into a __sizzling **(1)**__ ball of flames.

Write a sentence to end the diary entry.

Answers will vary. **(1)**
_____

Name _____

Selection Map

Fill in this selection map.

Pages 59–68

Page 59   Storm Chasing how Warren chases a lightning storm **(2 points)**

Page 60   Warren Faidley: Storm Chaser how Warren was
interested in storms since he was a child **(2)**

Page 64   What Happens to Warren's Photos After He Takes Them?
how Warren created a stock photo agency, where
people can go and buy his photos **(2)**

Page 65   Storm Seasons and Chasing how tornadoes form and how storm
chasers follow weather patterns that form tornadoes **(2)**

Page 67   Chasing Tornadoes how Warren knows where to go to get the best
pictures of tornadoes **(2)**

Pages 69–75

One Day in the Life of a Storm Chaser

Morning Check the weather, get Shadow Chaser
ready for the day, test the equipment, pack supplies **(2 points)**

Afternoon Get an update on the weather conditions, change the
oil in Shadow Chaser, check maps **(2)**

Evening Look at the map, call the National Weather Service,
head north following the storm, follow the tornadoes from
Texas into Oklahoma, shoot the photos **(2)**

Assessment Tip: Total **16** Points

Name _____

An Interview with Warren Faidley

The questions below can be used to interview Warren Faidley about his life and work. Write the answer Warren might give to each question.

What is your occupation?
I chase tornadoes, hurricanes, and lightning storms and try to
photograph them. I sell my pictures through my stock photo agency. **(2 points)**

When did you first become interested in storms? Describe one of your early experiences with storms. I've been interested in storms since
I was a boy. One time I rode my bike into the middle of a dust whirlwind. **(2)**

What led you to become a professional storm chaser? I was working
for a newspaper. I had a hobby, which was taking photos of lightning
from my balcony. During one particular storm, I chased a dark
thundercloud and managed to get an astonishing picture of a lightning
bolt hitting a pole. I realized I could sell photos of storms, so I started
a stock photo agency. **(2)**

How important is it for someone in your line of work to have a good knowledge of weather patterns? Why? It's very important, because
weather patterns cause storms, and the same patterns occur in the
same places every year. Knowing about storm patterns tells a storm
chaser where to go, and when. **(2)**

What advice would you give a young person who wants to become a storm chaser? Possible response: Be patient. Be careful. **(2)**

Text Tracking

Read the article below. Then complete the activity on page 35.

Hurricane Basics

A hurricane is a powerful storm with swirling winds. Hurricanes form over water in tropical parts of the North Atlantic and North Pacific Oceans. Most hurricanes in these regions occur between June and November.

Rise of a Hurricane

A hurricane does not form all at once. First, areas of low pressure develop in ocean winds. These areas, called easterly waves, then grow into a tropical depression, where winds blow at up to 31 miles per hour. As the winds pick up speed, they become a tropical storm. Finally, when the winds reach 74 miles per hour or more, and the storm is 200 to 300 miles wide, it is considered a hurricane.

Path of Destruction

The great speed of a hurricane's winds can cause severe damage. A hurricane can destroy buildings and other property when it reaches land. The force of these winds can also create huge waves. The waves along with the heavy rains may cause flooding in rivers and low-lying coastal lands. Many hurricane deaths are the result of flooding. Because of the devastating power of hurricanes, meteorologists keep a close watch on the Pacific and Atlantic Oceans during hurricane season.

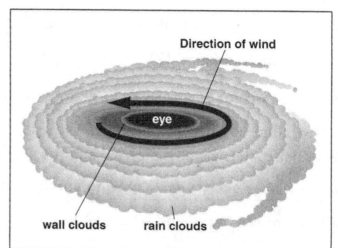

The winds of a hurricane rotate around the eye, which is an area of calm in the storm's center. Wall clouds surround the eye.

Name _____

Text Tracking continued

Write words from the box to indicate the order in which these parts appear in the article on page 34. Then answer the questions.

> caption   graphic aid   headings   introduction

1. introduction **(1 point)**

2. headings **(1)**

3. graphic aid **(1)**

4. caption **(1)**

5. What is each paragraph about?

   Paragraph 1:   what hurricanes are; where and when they form **(2)**

   Paragraph 2:   how hurricanes form **(2)**

   Paragraph 3:   the damage hurricanes can cause **(2)**

6. Is the information in paragraph 2 organized by main idea and details, or by sequence of events?   by sequence of events **(2)**

7. How is the information in paragraph 3 organized?   by main idea and details **(2)**

Name _____

Stormy Syllables

Write the underlined word using slash marks (/) between its syllables.
Then write a new sentence that uses the underlined word. Sample answers shown.

1. The photographer changed her <u>position</u> to get a better shot of the storm.
   po/si/tion **(1 point)** I moved the chair to a new position. **(2)**

2. A good photographer tries to <u>capture</u> the excitement of the moment.
   cap/ture **(1)** I tried to capture a butterfly in my net. **(2)**

3. Warren showed exciting <u>videos</u> of tornadoes. vi/de/os **(1)**
   We watched three videos over the weekend. **(2)**

4. I <u>wonder</u> how she was able to get so close to the lightning bolt.
   won/der **(1)** I wonder where we will go on our vacation. **(2)**

5. By <u>rotating</u> his body, he could follow the circular path of the tornado.
   ro/tat/ing **(1)** The moon is rotating around Earth. **(2)**

Name _____

The /ā/, /ē/, and /ī/ Sounds

When you hear the /ā/ sound, think of the patterns
a-consonant-*e*, *ai*, and *ay*. When you hear the /ē/ sound, think of
the patterns *ea* and *ee*. When you hear the /ī/ sound, think of the
patterns i-consonant-*e*, *igh*, and *i*.

/ā/	**fade claim stray**
/ē/	**leaf speech**
/ī/	**strike thigh sign**

► The long vowel sounds in the starred words have different
spelling patterns. The /ē/ sound in *thief* and in *niece* is spelled *ie*.
The /ī/ sound in *height* is spelled *eigh*.

Write each Spelling Word under its vowel sound.
Order of answers for each category may vary.

/ā/	/ē/	/ī/
claim **(1 point)**	speech **(1)**	strike **(1)**
stray **(1)**	leaf **(1)**	sign **(1)**
fade **(1)**	thief **(1)**	thigh **(1)**
waist **(1)**	beast **(1)**	height **(1)**
sway **(1)**	fleet **(1)**	mild **(1)**
stain **(1)**	niece **(1)**	stride **(1)**
praise **(1)**		slight **(1)**

Spelling Words

1. speech
2. claim
3. strike
4. stray
5. fade
6. sign
7. leaf
8. thigh
9. thief*
10. height*
11. mild
12. waist
13. sway
14. beast
15. stain
16. fleet
17. stride
18. praise
19. slight
20. niece*

Name _____

Spelling Spree

Find a Rhyme For each sentence write a Spelling Word that rhymes with the underlined word and makes sense in the sentence.

1. On what <u>day</u> did you last see the stray **(1 point)** cat?

2. It looks like the stain **(1)** got washed out by the <u>rain</u>.

3. She liked to stride **(1)** down the beach at low <u>tide</u>.

4. They swam out to <u>meet</u> the fleet **(1)** of ships.

5. How <u>high</u> on the thigh **(1)** did the ball hit you?

6. His niece **(1)** asked for another <u>piece</u> of pie.

7. The police <u>chief</u> took credit for catching the thief **(1)** .

8. The young <u>child</u> liked mild **(1)** food better than spicy food.

Crack the Code Some Spelling Words have been written in the code below. Use the code to figure out each word. Then write the word correctly. (**1 point** each)

CODE:	R	V	L	O	C	A	D	X	P	T	Y	Q	J	N	E	I	M
LETTER:	a	b	c	e	f	g	h	i	l	m	n	p	r	s	t	w	y

9. LPRXT claim

10. IRXNE waist

11. VORNE beast

12. NQOOLD speech

13. NXAY sign

14. DOXADE height

15. NPXADE slight

16. NIRM sway

17. QJRXNO praise

18. PORC leaf

Spelling Words

1. speech
2. claim
3. strike
4. stray
5. fade
6. sign
7. leaf
8. thigh
9. thief*
10. height*
11. mild
12. waist
13. sway
14. beast
15. stain
16. fleet
17. stride
18. praise
19. slight
20. niece*

Name _____

Proofreading and Writing

Proofreading Circle the five misspelled Spelling Words in this weather log entry. Then write each word correctly.

May 20 — There was a report today of a lightning (streik) at the shopping mall outside town. The same storm passed over our house, with heavy winds. It made the trees (sweigh) so much that I was sure at least one would fall. The winds started to (faide) before that happened, though. On the news, the reporter said that the base of the storm clouds was actually at a (hight) of over 5,000 feet. The weather tomorrow is supposed to be mild, with a (slite) chance of rain.

1. speech
2. claim
3. strike
4. stray
5. fade
6. sign
7. leaf
8. thigh
9. thief*
10. height*
11. mild
12. waist
13. sway
14. beast
15. stain
16. fleet
17. stride
18. praise
19. slight
20. niece*

1. strike **(1 point)**

2. sway **(1)**

3. fade **(1)**

4. height **(1)**

5. slight **(1)**

▬▬ **Write a Storm Warning** Storm chasers are able to provide firsthand, "you are there" reports of storms because they chase the storms.

On a separate sheet of paper, write the script of a storm warning that a storm chaser might issue by radio. Use Spelling Words from the list. Responses will vary. **(5 points)**

Words in Their Places

Read each set of words, and decide which two could be the guide words and which one the entry word on a dictionary page. Then in the columns below, write the guide words under the correct heading, and the entry word beside them.

trout trust tropical	weather wayward weave	prance practice prairie	durable dust dusky	chase charter chatterbox

Guide Words		Entry Word
tropical (**1**)	trust (**1**)	trout (**1**)
wayward (**1**)	weave (**1**)	weather (**1**)
practice (**1**)	prance (**1**)	prairie (**1**)
durable (**1**)	dust (**1**)	dusky (**1**)
charter (**1**)	chatterbox (**1**)	chase (**1**)

Name _____

It's a Twister!

Conjunctions The words *and, or,* and *but* are **conjunctions**. A conjunction may be used to join words in a sentence or to join sentences. Use *and* to add information. Use *or* to give a choice. Use *but* to show contrast.

■ Clouds **and** wind signal a coming storm.
  This conjunction joins words.
■ I saw lightning, **and** I heard thunder.
  This conjunction joins sentences.

Write the conjunction *and, or,* or *but* to best complete each sentence. Then decide whether each conjunction you wrote joins words or joins sentences. Write W after a sentence in which words are joined. Write S after a sentence in which sentences are joined.

1. Kansas _and_ Oklahoma have many tornadoes. _W_ **(2 points)**

2. Warren Faidley chases tornadoes _or/and_ thunderstorms. _W_ **(2)**

3. Warren has special equipment, _and_ he has a special vehicle to carry it. _S_ **(2)**

4. I have never seen a tornado, _but_ I have seen lightning many times. _S_ **(2)**

5. Go into a cellar _or_ another low place if you see a funnel cloud. _W_ **(2)**

Name _____

In Focus

Compound Sentences A **compound sentence** is made by joining two closely related simple sentences with a comma and a conjunction.

I like to read.
You like to write. } I like to read, but you like to write.

Draw a line from each simple sentence in column A to the most closely related sentence in column B. Read all the choices before you decide. Answers may vary. (**1 point** for each line.)

A	B
1. Zoe takes photos for the school paper	Zoe took pictures of the musicians.
2. Should Zoe use color film	Tom writes stories for the paper.
3. Color photos are nice	the photos in our newspaper are black and white.
4. Tom wrote about the school concert	should she use black and white film?

Now, write the sentences above and join them by using conjunctions instead of lines. Don't forget to put a comma before each conjunction!

1. Zoe takes photos for the school paper, and Tom writes stories for the paper. **(1)**

2. Should Zoe use color film, or should she use black and white film? **(1)**

3. Color photos are nice, but the photos in our newspaper are black and white. **(1)**

4. Tom wrote about the school concert, and Zoe took pictures of the musicians. **(1)**

42   Theme 1: **Nature's Fury**
Assessment Tip: Total **8** Points

Name _____

Lightning Strikes!

Correcting Run-on Sentences A **run-on sentence** occurs when a writer
runs one simple sentence into another without using a comma and a
conjunction between them. The sentence below is a run-on sentence.

Marco lives on a farm his cousin likes to visit him there.

Correct run-on sentences in your writing by inserting a comma and
conjunction to make a compound sentence:

, and
Marco lives on a farm his cousin likes to visit him there.
        ^

**Marco is excited and has quickly typed an e-mail message to his
cousin Jamie. Revise Marco's message by adding missing
commas and conjunctions. (2 points each)**

, and
Lightning struck near our farm I saw
                          ^
it happen. The bolt hit an old tree on
                    and
top of a hill, the tree split in half.
            ^
                 , and
There was a loud boom the air
                    ^
                , but
crackle. It was scary I was safe in
                      ^
our house at the bottom of the hill.

Should I send you a picture of the
     , or
tree do you want to visit to see it for
    ^
yourself?

Name _____

Responding to a Prompt

A **prompt** is a direction that asks for a written answer of one or more
paragraphs. Read the following prompts.

Prompt 1

What job do you think is the
most difficult or dangerous?
Explain why you think it is
difficult or dangerous.

Prompt 2

Think about how Warren Faidley
customized Shadow Chaser for
chasing tornadoes. Describe how
you would customize a vehicle for a
specific task.

**Choose one prompt and use the chart below to help you write a
response. First, list key words in the prompt. Then jot down main
ideas and details you might include. Finally, number your main ideas,
beginning with *1*, from most to least important.**

Key Words	Main Ideas	Details
Prompt 1: explain **(1 point)** Prompt 2: describe	(2)	(2)

**Write your response on a separate sheet of paper. Start by restating
the prompt. Then write your main ideas and supporting details in
order of importance from most to least important, or from least to
most important. (5)**

44   Theme 1: **Nature's Fury**
Assessment Tip: Total **10** Points

Name _____

Capitalizing and Punctuating Sentences

A fifth-grade class was given this writing prompt: **Warren Faidley is a storm chaser. Summarize what he does for a living.** One fifth grader wrote the response below but forgot to check for capitalization and punctuation errors.

Use these proofreading marks to add the necessary capital letters and end punctuation. (1 point each)

⊙ Add a period.   ∧! Add an exclamation point.

≡ Make a capital letter.   ∧? Add a question mark.

what does Warren Faidley do for a living? He follows dangerous storms⊙
for example, he tracks down tornadoes and hurricanes⊙then he
photographs lightning striking the earth and funnel clouds whirling in
the sky. if he has been successful, he can sell his dramatic photos to
magazines, newspapers, and other publications⊙What a risky but
exciting job storm chasers have !

Name _____

Volcanic Activity

Write each word from the box under the correct category below.

Description of Hot Lava
molten (**1 point**)
_____

Earth Layer
crust (**1**)
_____

Materials in a Volcano
lava (**1**)
_____

magma (**1**)
_____

cinders (**1**)
_____

Volcano Parts
crater (**1**)
_____

summit (**1**)
_____

Event
eruption (**1**)
_____

Vocabulary

molten

lava

crater

crust

cinders

eruption

magma

summit

Now choose at least four words from the box. Use them to write a short paragraph describing an exploding volcano.

(1 point for each word)

_____
_____
_____
_____
_____

46   Theme 1: **Nature's Fury**
Assessment Tip: Total **12** Points

Name _____

Category Chart

Fill in the boxes in each category.

How Volcanoes Form

Magma pushes up through vents or cracks in the earth's crust. **(1 point)**

_____

Two Types of Volcanic Vents

a hole in the ground that lava

flows from **(1)**

_____

a mountain or hill that lava flows

from **(1)**

_____

Where Volcanoes Form

Most volcanoes form where the plates of the earth come together. Hawaiian

volcanoes are in the middle of the Pacific plate. **(1)**

Types of Volcanoes

shield volcanoes **(1)**	cinder cone volcanoes **(1)**	composite volcanoes **(1)**	dome volcanoes **(1)**
examples Mauna Loa Kilauea **(1)**	**examples** some volcanoes in Guatemala **(1)**	**examples** Mount Shasta Mount Hood **(1)**	**examples** Lassen Peak **(1)**

Name _____

Show What You Know!

The following questions ask about volcanoes. Answer each question by writing the letter of the correct answer in the space provided.

B (1) ___ 1. Where does the word *volcano* come from?

A. the Hawaiian name for the goddess of fire, Pele

B. the name for the Roman god of fire, Vulcan

C. the scientific name for mountains that spout fire and ash

D. the name for a race of mythological creatures called Vulcans

A (1) ___ 2. How are volcanoes formed?

A. Hot magma beneath the earth's crust pushes up through cracks or holes.

B. The earth's crust melts and forms rivers of hot lava.

C. Wood and other materials catch fire and cause explosions that melt mountaintops.

D. Glaciers melt, leaving craters through which magma can escape.

B (1) ___ 3. What happened when Mt. St. Helens erupted in 1980?

A. The first of the Hawaiian islands was formed in the Pacific Ocean.

B. Homes, roads, and forests were destroyed, and 60 people were killed.

C. Ash spewed into the air, but no real damage was done.

D. A new volcanic island appeared in the North Atlantic Ocean.

D (1) ___ 4. Where in the earth's crust do most volcanoes erupt?

A. in the weakest parts of the earth's plates, near the center

B. in the Atlantic Ocean

C. wherever mountains or mountain ranges are found

D. in places where two of the earth's plates meet

C (1) ___ 5. How have volcanoes helped to create the Hawaiian Islands?

A. Eruptions destroyed much of the land area, leaving only islands.

B. Eruptions caught the attention of explorers, who settled there.

C. Eruptions built up the islands, and new eruptions add lava to the shoreline.

D. Ash and cinders from thousands of eruptions have mixed with seawater to help form new land.

Assessment Tip: Total **5** Points

Name _____

Classifying Clouds

Read the article. Then complete the activity on page 50.

Clouds

Clouds come in a variety of forms and colors. They occur at different heights. Some are made of water and some of ice. With all these differences, a good way to identify clouds is by their groups.

Clouds are grouped by how high above the earth they are found. Low clouds are usually not more than 6,000 feet above sea level. They include stratus and stratocumulus clouds. A stratus cloud looks like a smooth sheet, while stratocumulus clouds are lumpy. They look like fluffy gray piles of cotton.

Middle clouds form between 6,000 and 20,000 feet. They include altostratus, altocumulus, and nimbostratus clouds. An altostratus cloud forms a white or gray sheet. Altocumulus clouds appear as fluffy piles that may be separated or connected in a lumpy mass. Nimbostratus clouds look like a smooth, gray layer. Rain or snow often falls from them, making them hard to see.

High clouds form above 20,000 feet. Unlike other kinds of clouds, which are made of water droplets, these clouds consist of ice crystals. Cirrus, cirrostratus, and cirrocumulus are types of high clouds. Cirrus clouds are very high in the sky and have a feathery appearance. A cirrostratus cloud is a very thin cloud layer. Cirrocumulus clouds look like millions of bits of fluff high in the sky.

Name _____

Classifying Clouds continued

Follow the directions or answer the questions based on the article.

1. Add the names of any cloud types mentioned in the article that are missing from this chart.

low	middle	high
stratus	altostratus	cirrus
stratocumulus **(1 point)**	altocumulus **(1)**	cirrostratus **(1)**
	nimbostratus **(1)**	cirrocumulus **(1)**

2. How are the clouds in this chart classified? by shape or appearance **(2)**
   Write the correct category for each list of clouds in this chart.

sheet or layer **(1)**	fluffy **(1)**
stratus	stratocumulus
altostratus	altocumulus
nimbostratus	cirrocumulus
cirrostratus	

3. How are the clouds in this chart classified? by what they are made of **(2)**
   Add the names of cloud types not listed to the correct column.

water	ice
stratus	cirrus
altostratus	cirrostratus
nimbostratus	cirrocumulus **(1)**
stratocumulus **(1)**	
altocumulus **(1)**	

Assessment Tip: Total **14** Points

Name _____

Construct a Word

Read each sentence. Then, using two or three columns in the chart, build a word containing the root -*struct* or -*rupt* that completes the sentence. Write the word on the line.

de	rupt	ive
dis	struct	or
con		ion
e		ure
inter		
in		

1. Sam's swimming <u>instructor **(1 point)**</u>

   taught him how to do the backstroke.

2. I watched the <u>eruption **(1)**</u> of the

   volcano from my window.

3. We helped our cousin <u>construct **(1)**</u> a tree house

   in the backyard.

4. The hurricane left a path of <u>destruction **(1)**</u>

   along the coast.

5. Please don't <u>interrupt **(1)**</u> me when

   I'm talking!

6. The noise in the hall was very <u>disruptive **(1)**</u>

   during our rehearsal.

7. The leak was caused by a <u>rupture **(1)**</u>

   in the pipeline.

8. The children sat on top of the climbing

   <u>structure **(1)**</u> in the playground.

Name _____

The /ō/, /o͞o/, and /yo͞o/ Sounds

When you hear the /ō/ sound, think of the patterns *o*-consonant-*e*, *oa*, *ow*, and *o*. When you hear the /o͞o/ and the /yo͞o/ sounds, think of the patterns *u*-consonant-*e*, *ue*, *ew*, *oo*, *ui*, and *ou*. Order of answers for each category may vary.

/ō/ **slope, boast, thrown, stroll**

/o͞o/ or /yo͞o/ **rule, clue, dew, choose, cruise, route**

Write each Spelling Word under its vowel sound.

/ō/ Sound

thrown **(1 point)**   loaf **(1)**

stole **(1)**   growth **(1)**

boast **(1)**   slope **(1)**

stroll **(1)**   flow **(1)**

/o͞o/ or /yo͞o/ Sounds

clue **(1)**   mood **(1)**

dew **(1)**   youth **(1)**

choose **(1)**   bruise **(1)**

rule **(1)**   loose **(1)**

cruise **(1)**   rude **(1)**

route **(1)**   flute **(1)**

Spelling Words

1. thrown
2. stole
3. clue
4. dew
5. choose
6. rule
7. boast
8. cruise
9. stroll
10. route
11. mood
12. loaf
13. growth
14. youth
15. slope
16. bruise
17. loose
18. rude
19. flow
20. flute

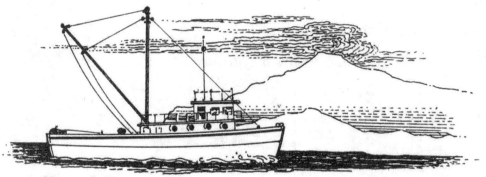

52   Theme 1: **Nature's Fury**
Assessment Tip: Total **20 Points**

Name _____

Spelling Spree

Letter Swap Write a Spelling Word by changing the underlined letter to a different letter.

1. st<u>a</u>le   stole **(1 point)**

2. lo<u>u</u>se   loose **(1)**

3. clu<u>b</u>   clue **(1)**

4. loa<u>d</u>   loaf **(1)**

5. r<u>o</u>le   rule **(1)**

6. <u>t</u>oast   boast **(1)**

7. moo<u>n</u>   mood **(1)**

8. de<u>n</u>   dew **(1)**

1. thrown
2. stole
3. clue
4. dew
5. choose
6. rule
7. boast
8. cruise
9. stroll
10. route
11. mood
12. loaf
13. growth
14. youth
15. slope
16. bruise
17. loose
18. rude
19. flow
20. flute

Word Switch Write a Spelling Word to replace each underlined definition in the sentences. Write your words on the lines.

9. My parents are taking a <u>sea voyage for pleasure</u> on that ship.

10. Which item did you <u>pick out</u> from the catalog?

11. Many people are active in sports in their <u>time of life before adulthood</u>.

12. You can use a ruler to measure the <u>increase in size</u> of the plant.

13. I play the <u>woodwind instrument shaped like a tube</u> in the band.

14. A clerk should never be <u>lacking in courtesy</u> to a shopper.

15. Would you care to <u>walk slowly</u> down the beach with me?

9. cruise **(1)**

10. choose **(1)**

11. youth **(1)**

12. growth **(1)**

13. flute **(1)**

14. rude **(1)**

15. stroll **(1)**

Name _____

Proofreading and Writing

Proofreading Circle the five misspelled Spelling Words in this paragraph from a personal narrative. Then write each word correctly.

Spelling Words

Our (roote) led us up the side of the volcano. We had just reached an old area of lava (flo) when we heard a rumbling noise from above. Hikers ahead of us on the trail had knocked some rocks loose! The avalanche was heading down the (sloap) of the mountain, straight for us. In the rush to reach safety, I tripped and was (thron) off the trail. Luckily, the mass of rocks passed me by, and all I got was a (briuse) on my leg.

1. route **(2 points)**
2. flow **(2)**
3. slope **(2)**
4. thrown **(2)**
5. bruise **(2)**

Spelling Words

1. thrown
2. stole
3. clue
4. dew
5. choose
6. rule
7. boast
8. cruise
9. stroll
10. route
11. mood
12. loaf
13. growth
14. youth
15. slope
16. bruise
17. loose
18. rude
19. flow
20. flute

✏️➤ **Write a List of Safety Tips** What safety tips would it be good to keep in mind when exploring a volcano?

On a separate sheet of paper, list some tips for volcano explorers. Use Spelling Words from the list. Responses will vary. **(5 points)**

Assessment Tip: Total **15** Points

Name _____

Missing Definitions

The dictionary entries below include an entry word and a sample sentence, but they are missing the definition. Read each sample sentence and use it to help you fill in the definition.

Accept any reasonable answer. Sample answers shown.

1. ancient (ān′ shənt) Very old **(2 points)**

   The dinosaur tracks in the rocks show how ancient they are.

2. astonishing (ə **stŏn′** ĭ shĭng) Surprising **(2)**

   It was astonishing to see it snowing in the middle of July.

3. awaken (ə **wā′** kən) To wake up **(2)**

   The campers awaken at the first light of dawn.

4. damage (**dăm′** ĭj) To harm or hurt **(2)**

   Using too much water can damage the plants.

5. extinct (ĭk **stĭngkt′**) No longer active **(2)**

   Since its last eruption a thousand years ago, the volcano has been extinct.

6. fiery (**fīr′** ē) Like fire; made of fire **(2)**

   The flames made a fiery glow in the sky.

7. spout (spout) To gush or spurt out **(2)**

   Water from the fountain spouts into the air.

8. summit (**sŭm′** ĭt) The highest point; peak **(2)**

   After a long hard climb, we reached the summit of the mountain.

Name _____

Finding Your Way

Singular and Plural Nouns A **singular noun** names one person, one place, one thing, or one idea. A **plural noun** names more than one person, place, thing, or idea. To decide how to form a plural, look at the end of the singular noun. Here are four rules to study:

1. To most singular nouns, add *-s* to form the plural.
2. If a singular noun ends in *s*, *ss*, *x*, *ch*, or *sh*, add *-es* to form the plural.
3. For singular nouns ending with a vowel plus *y*, add *-s* to form the plural.
4. If a singular noun ends in a consonant plus *y*, change the *y* to *i* and add *-es*.

bench
table
tree
fox
fireplace
tent
daisy
bush
bus
pathway

Conrad and Carmen have drawn a map of a campground they are visiting. Label each landmark on the map with a plural noun. Use nouns from the list. (1 point each)

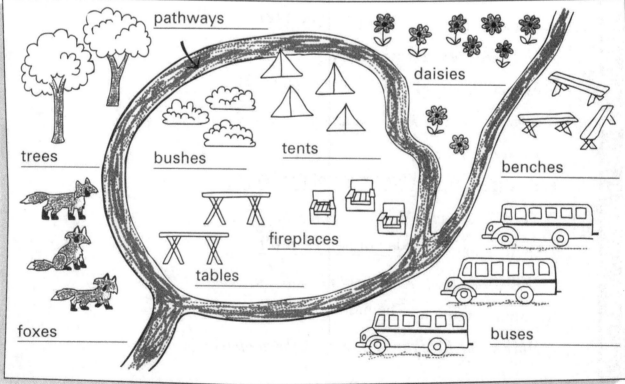

Assessment Tip: Total **10** Points

Name _____

Science Fair

More Plural Nouns Here are a few more rules for forming plurals:

1. To form the plural of some nouns ending in *f* or *fe*, change the *f* to *v* and add *-es*. For others ending in *f*, simply add *-s*.
2. To form the plural of nouns ending with a vowel plus *o*, add *-s*.
3. To form the plural of nouns ending with a consonant plus *o*, add *-s* or *-es*.
4. Some nouns have special plural forms.
5. Some nouns are the same in the singular and the plural.

For the science fair, Jody made a model of the volcano Mount Saint Helens and wrote a report about it. Jody isn't sure how to form the plural of some words in her report. She made a list of these words.

Write the plural next to each word on Jody's list. Check your dictionary if you are unsure of a plural.

leaf	leaves **(1 point)**
child	children **(1)**
volcano	volcanoes **(1)**
man	men **(1)**
ash	ashes **(1)**
home	homes **(1)**
deer	deer **(1)**
woman	women **(1)**
plant	plants **(1)**
mouse	mice **(1)**

Assessment Tip: Total **10** Points

Name _____

Roaming Through the Woods

Using Exact Nouns You can make your writing more lively and interesting by replacing general nouns with more specific ones. Here is an example of writing with a general noun:

For my birthday, I received **several things**.

A reader does not know what the person received. Here is the same sentence revised to use more specific nouns:

For my birthday, I received **a book about sports legends, a basketball, and basketball shoes.**

Read the following paragraph. Revise the general nouns in bold type by replacing them with a more specific noun from the box. (1 point each)

> a rabbit
> dragonfly
> maples and oaks
> Duck Pond
> minnows
> peanut butter
> sandwiches
> my ankles
> mint
> bark
> sneakers

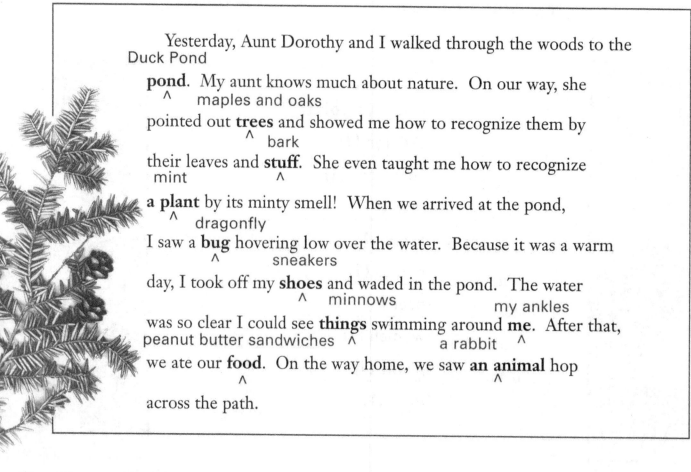

>   Yesterday, Aunt Dorothy and I walked through the woods to the
> Duck Pond
> **pond**. My aunt knows much about nature. On our way, she
>   ^   maples and oaks
> pointed out **trees** and showed me how to recognize them by
>   ^ bark
> their leaves and **stuff**. She even taught me how to recognize
>   mint   ^
> **a plant** by its minty smell! When we arrived at the pond,
>   ^   dragonfly
> I saw a **bug** hovering low over the water. Because it was a warm
>   ^   sneakers
> day, I took off my **shoes** and waded in the pond. The water
>   ^ minnows
>   my ankles
> was so clear I could see **things** swimming around **me**. After that,
> peanut butter sandwiches ^   a rabbit ^
> we ate our **food**. On the way home, we saw **an animal** hop
>   ^   ^
> across the path.

Name _____

Writing a Paragraph of Information

Read the following paragraph of information from page 87 of *Volcanoes*.

   Volcanoes are formed by cracks or holes that poke through the earth's crust. Magma pushes its way up through the cracks. This is called a volcanic eruption. When magma pours onto the surface it is called lava. . . . As lava cools, it hardens to form rock.

Now get ready to write your own paragraph of information about volcanoes. Use the following graphic organizer to help you organize your paragraph. (5 points)

Topic

Topic Sentence

Supporting Sentences

Now, write your paragraph of information on a separate sheet of paper. Arrange your supporting sentences in a logical order, and make sure all of the sentences contain facts about the topic. (5 points)

Name _____

Correcting Sentence Fragments

**A sentence fragment is a group of words that is missing either a
subject or a predicate. The following groups of words are sentence
fragments. Turn them into complete sentences by adding either
a subject or a predicate. Write the complete sentence
on the lines.** Responses will vary.

1. Many of the world's active volcanoes.

   Many of the world's active volcanoes are destructive. **(3 points)**

   _____

2. Clouds of hot ash.

   Clouds of hot ash fill the air. **(3)**

   _____

3. Buries plants and animals.

   Quick-moving lava buries plants and animals. **(3)**

   _____

4. The blast of an eruption.

   The blast of an eruption topples trees and buildings. **(3)**

   _____

5. Are seriously injured or killed.

   Hundreds of people are seriously injured or killed. **(3)**

   _____

Assessment Tip: Total **15** Points

Name _____

Tornado Report

Use the words in the box to complete this news report about a tornado.

Vocabulary

alert   flickering   reception   bolting   lull   huddled

A Category 4 tornado touched down in central Nebraska at approximately 4:30 P.M. yesterday. A severe weather
alert **(2 points)** _____ was issued by the National Weather Service before the storm struck. However, many residents lost power and had no reception **(2)** _____ on their radios or televisions at the time.

Witnesses who still had power reported that their lights were flickering **(2)** _____ on and off as the twister approached. One man remembered bolting **(2)** _____ for the basement of his house as he heard the storm draw nearer. A local woman recalled a period of absolute stillness right before the tornado hit. During this
lull **(2)** _____, she wondered if the tornado had passed by. Most local residents huddled **(2)** _____ in the center of their basements until the storm passed, following safety guidelines published in yesterday's newspaper.

Name _____

Storm Sequences

Wording of answers may vary.

	Night of the Twisters	Blizzard!
First, a storm	causes a tornado that is heading toward Dan's house **(1 point)**	brings a lot of snow and freezes the East River **(1)**
The people in the selection go	down into the house's basement **(1)**	out onto the frozen river **(1)**
Then,	they huddle in the basement while the tornado destroys the house **(1)**	the river starts to break up and people get stuck on the ice **(1)**
At the end of the selection,	Dan, Arthur, and Ryan are scared but okay. **(1)**	everyone has been rescued from the ice floes **(1)**

Assessment Tip: Total **8** Points

Describing Twisters

Compare and contrast the descriptions of tornadoes in *Night of the Twisters* and *Eye of the Storm*. Use the categories on the chart to list details from each selection. Sample answers are shown.

	Night of the Twisters	*Eye of the Storm*
Vivid verbs	howling; shrieking; whining **(2 points)**	stretch; wiggling; swirling; sucking **(2)**
Sensory details	I felt the wall shudder behind us **(2)**	edges of storm cloud wrap around the tornado, hiding it from sight **(2)**
Figurative language	bearing down on us like a hundred freight trains **(2)**	it looks like the trunk of a huge elephant; like a long stovepipe **(2)**

Assessment Tip: Total **12** Points

Name _____

Emergency Response Words

Write each word from the box in the space next to its meaning.

Vocabulary

| immense | treacherous | desperate |
| ominous | stranded | floes |

1. unable to reach safety <u>stranded **(1 point)**</u>

2. very, very dangerous <u>treacherous **(1)**</u>

3. frantic and willing to try anything <u>desperate **(1)**</u>

4. chunks of floating ice <u>floes **(1)**</u>

5. signaling danger or trouble <u>ominous **(1)**</u>

6. huge <u>immense **(1)**</u>

Now choose four words from the box. Use them to write a short paragraph describing a winter storm you have experienced or read about. <u>Answers will vary, but should include four vocabulary words.</u>

(1 point for each word used correctly.)

_____

_____

_____

_____

_____

Assessment Tip: Total **10** Points

Name _____

Test Practice

Use the three steps you've learned to choose the best answer for these questions about *Blizzard!* **Fill in the circle for the best answer in the answer row at the bottom of the page.**

1. Why did the author write about the ice floes in *Blizzard!*?

   A to compare different types of natural disasters

   B to tell a true story about a dangerous situation

   C to explain how to cross ice floes safely

   D to persuade people not to cross frozen rivers

2. Why did ladder operators raise their prices when they saw the tugboats?

   F because people would soon need to leave the ice

   G because people would want to come see the tugboats

   H because crossing on broken ice would be more exciting

   J because people would want to ride on the tugboats

3. What caused the ice to begin moving toward the sea?

   A the weight of the people   **C** the windy conditions

   B the shifting of the tide   **D** the heavy snowfall

4. **Connecting/Comparing** In what way are the people who walked onto the ice different from storm chasers such as Warren in *Eye of the Storm*?

   F The people on the ice used special equipment.

   G The people on the ice were scientists.

   H Storm chasers' work is not helpful to others.

   J Storm chasers weigh the dangers before acting.

ANSWER ROWS   1 Ⓐ ⬤Ⓑ Ⓒ Ⓓ **(5 points)**   3 Ⓐ ⬤Ⓑ Ⓒ Ⓓ **(5)**

2 ⬤Ⓕ Ⓖ Ⓗ Ⓙ **(5)**   4 Ⓕ Ⓖ Ⓗ ⬤Ⓙ **(5)**

Continue on page 66.

Theme 1: **Nature's Fury**   65

Name _____

Test Practice continued

5. Why did most people ignore the police?

    A They did not like figures of authority.

    B They did not care about safety.

    C They were eager for adventure.

    D They did not understand the police.

6. Who provided most of the first-hand information about the rescue of the floaters?

    F the author

    G a policeman

    H one of the rescued men

    J a newspaper reporter

7. Why do you think the spectators cheered after the last floaters were rescued?

    A They enjoyed the drama.

    B They were relieved everyone was safe.

    C They admired the tugboats.

    D They admired the floaters.

8. **Connecting/Comparing** In what way was the family dog in *Earthquake Terror* like the dogs in *Blizzard!*?

    F Both dogs sensed danger.

    G Both dogs protected people.

    H Both dogs barked warnings.

    J Both dogs rescued others.

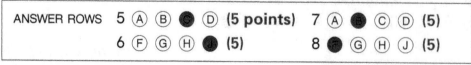

ANSWER ROWS 5 Ⓐ Ⓑ ● Ⓓ **(5 points)** 7 Ⓐ ● Ⓒ Ⓓ **(5)**
6 Ⓕ Ⓖ Ⓗ ● **(5)** 8 ● Ⓖ Ⓗ Ⓙ **(5)**

Assessment Tip: Total **40** Points

Name _____

How Is It Organized?

Read the article. Then complete the activity below.

Tsunamis[1]

   A tsunami (tsoo NAH mee)[2] is a giant ocean wave produced by an undersea earthquake, landslide, or volcanic eruption. Most tsunamis occur in the Pacific Ocean. The wave may only be a few feet high in the open ocean, but as it approaches a coastline it can rise to a height of over 100 feet. How fast a tsunami travels depends on the depth of the water it is traveling through. In deep waters, a tsunami can travel 600 miles per hour. As it nears shore, however, the wave might slow to about 100 miles per hour.

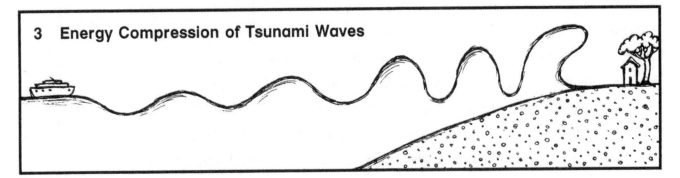

3   Energy Compression of Tsunami Waves

Use a word or phrase in the box to label each of the numbered text features in the article. Write your responses on the lines below.

1. title **(2 points)** _____

2. pronunciation key **(2)** _____

3. diagram **(2)** _____

┌─────────────────────┐
│ diagram   │
│ pronunciation key   │
│ title   │
└─────────────────────┘

Answer the questions.

4. What is the heading of the diagram?
   Energy Compression of Tsunami Waves **(2)** _____

5. How is the information in the article organized?
   by main idea and details **(2)** _____

Name _____

Earth Waves

Read the article. Then complete the activity below.

Earthquakes and Seismic Waves

An earthquake occurs when huge masses of rock shift and break below and on the surface of the earth. This movement releases energy that travels in all directions in the form of vibrations called seismic waves. These waves are classified according to how they travel. Fast vibrations known as **body waves** move through the earth. Slower **surface waves** move along the earth's surface.

Body waves travel faster deep within the earth than near the earth's surface. However, body waves usually cause the most damage during an earthquake. As body waves pass through the earth, they cause rock to move in different ways. One type of body wave, known as a compressional wave, pushes and pulls the rock. Another type, called a shear wave, makes rocks move from side to side.

Surface waves are long, slow waves that usually cause little damage. The two main kinds of surface waves are Love waves and Rayleigh waves. Love waves move the ground from side to side. Rayleigh waves make the surface of the earth roll like waves on the ocean.

Answer the questions.

How are seismic waves classified?
according to how they travel **(2 points)**
_____

Add names or categories that are missing from this chart.

Types of Seismic Waves **(2)**		
Body	Surface **(2)**	
compressional **(2)** shear	Love Rayleigh **(2)**	

Assessment Tip: Total **10** Points

Name _____

Decide Where to Divide

Read each sentence. Rewrite the underlined word with a slash or slashes to divide the syllables. After the word, write which of the following patterns helped you decide where to divide.

VCCV	VCV (long first vowel)
CVVC	VCV (short first vowel)

1. The sunset <u>glimmered</u> orange on the sparkling waves.
   glim-mered, VCCV **(2 points)**

2. A <u>giant</u> wave gathered strength and smashed into the shore.
   gi-ant, CVVC **(2)**

3. A <u>funnel</u> cloud threatened to reach the ground.
   fun-nel, VCCV **(2)**

4. The family took <u>shelter</u> in their basement.
   shel-ter, VCCV **(2)**

5. The tornado left the house with several <u>broken</u> windows.
   bro-ken, VCV (long first vowel) **(2)**

6. The <u>reporter</u> wrote an eyewitness account of the storm.
   re-por-ter, VCV/VCCV (long first vowel) **(2)**

Name _____

Meaning Match

Read the definitions and the four sentences at the bottom of the page. In the blank space after each sentence, write the correct meaning for the underlined word.

fragment (frăg´ mənt) *n.* **1.** A piece or part broken off or separated from a whole: *She picked up a fragment of the broken plate.* **2.** Something incomplete or not finished. *The note contained only a sentence fragment.* —*v.* to break into pieces. *The thin ice will fragment at the slightest pressure.*

particular (pər tĭk´ yə lər) *adj.* **1.** Of or for a single person, group, or thing. *Each group did its particular job.* **2.** Unique; having to do only with a certain person or thing. *The dog has a particular whine when it is hungry.* **3.** Demanding close attention to detail. *My aunt is very particular about housekeeping.* —*n.* a single item, fact, or detail.

vent (vĕnt) n. An opening through which liquid or gas can pass through or escape. *Hot air from the dryer flows through a hose to a vent in the wall.* —*v.* to express; give utterance to. *People vented their frustrations about the long ticket lines.*

1. Ash, rock, and fumes spewed outward through a <u>vent</u> in the side of the volcano. An opening through which liquid or gas can pass through or escape. **(2 points)**

2. The blast left a <u>particular</u> track of devastation.
   Unique; having to do only with a certain person or thing. **(2)**

3. The eruption sent <u>fragments</u> of rock flying in all directions.
   Pieces or parts broken off or separated from a whole. **(2)**

4. Sam had to <u>vent</u> his anger that we were not taking the volcano threat seriously.
   To express. **(2)**

Assessment Tip: Total **8** Points

Name _____

Spelling Review

**Write Spelling Words from the list on this page to answer
the questions.**

Order of answers in each category may vary.

1–9. Which nine words have a short vowel sound?

1. fond **(1 point)**

2. swift **(1)**

3. slept **(1)**

4. staff **(1)**

5. grasp **(1)**

6. bunk **(1)**

7. dwell **(1)**

8. split **(1)**

9. crush **(1)**

10–19. Which ten words have the /ā/, /ē/, or /ī/ sound?

10. beast **(1)**

11. fleet **(1)**

12. thigh **(1)**

13. fade **(1)**

14. praise **(1)**

15. strike **(1)**

16. slight **(1)**

17. claim **(1)**

18. sway **(1)**

19. mild **(1)**

20–30. Which eleven words have the /ō/, /yo͞o/, or /o͞o/ sound?

20. flute **(1)**

21. dew **(1)**

22. clue **(1)**

23. slope **(1)**

24. boast **(1)**

25. stole **(1)**

26. stroll **(1)**

27. cruise **(1)**

28. mood **(1)**

29. youth **(1)**

30. thrown **(1)**

Spelling Words

1. fond
2. swift
3. beast
4. slept
5. fleet
6. staff
7. flute
8. grasp
9. thigh
10. dew
11. bunk
12. fade
13. dwell
14. strike
15. praise
16. slight
17. split
18. claim
19. sway
20. mild
21. clue
22. slope
23. boast
24. stole
25. stroll
26. cruise
27. mood
28. crush
29. youth
30. thrown

Assessment Tip: Total **30** Points

Spelling Spree

Puzzle Power Use the Spelling Words to complete the sentences. Write the words in the puzzle. (1 point each)

Across

3. The animals _____ in the forest.
5. A lion is a large _____.

Down

1. I am in a good _____ today.
2. The _____ is very steep.
4. Don't _____ that flower with your foot!

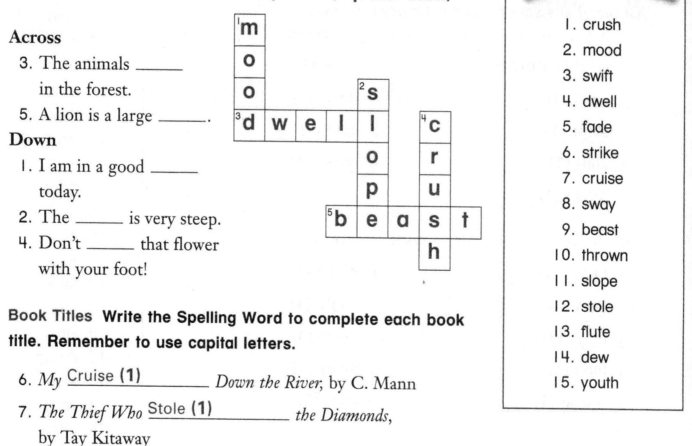

Spelling Words

1. crush
2. mood
3. swift
4. dwell
5. fade
6. strike
7. cruise
8. sway
9. beast
10. thrown
11. slope
12. stole
13. flute
14. dew
15. youth

Book Titles Write the Spelling Word to complete each book title. Remember to use capital letters.

6. *My* <u>Cruise **(1)**</u> *Down the River*, by C. Mann

7. *The Thief Who* <u>Stole **(1)**</u> *the Diamonds*, by Tay Kitaway

8. *The* <u>Swift **(1)**</u> *and Dangerous River*, by Can O. Tripp

9. *Earthquake:* <u>Thrown **(1)**</u> *to the Ground!* by Shay Keeg Round

10. *Why Do Colors* <u>Fade **(1)**</u> *in the Sun and Other Science Questions*, by Sy N. Tist

11. *Adventures of My Childhood and* <u>Youth **(1)**</u>, by A. Jing X. Plorer

12. *Flowers* <u>Sway **(1)**</u> *in the Breeze* by Heather Rose Marigold

13. *Mist in the Air,* <u>Dew **(1)**</u> *on the Grass* by I. M. Dampp

14. <u>Flute **(1)**</u> *Music for Beginners*, by Mary Days

15. *The Clock Will* <u>Strike **(1)**</u> *at Midnight*, by Miss Stear E. Yuss

Assessment Tip: Total **15** Points

Name _____

Proofreading and Writing

Proofreading Circle the six misspelled Spelling Words in this newspaper article. Then write each word correctly.

> At 11:30 last night, a (milde) earthquake gently rocked the city. Little damage was reported, and some people (sleept) right through it. This morning Helen and Joe Dalton (boste) that they were not afraid. There was only (slite) damage downtown. With (prayse) for his workers, the mayor said, "My (staf) responded quickly to all questions."

1. mild **(1 point)**

2. slept **(1)**

3. boast **(1)**

4. slight **(1)**

5. praise **(1)**

6. staff **(1)**

Spelling Words

1. slept
2. praise
3. fond
4. clue
5. staff
6. thigh
7. stroll
8. slight
9. claim
10. fleet
11. mild
12. grasp
13. split
14. bunk
15. boast

In the News A reporter takes notes after an earthquake. Complete his ideas by writing Spelling Words in the blanks.

- No one is <u>fond **(1)**</u> of surprises like this.

- Scientists have no <u>clue **(1)**</u> about why this quake occurred at night.

- It is a strange time to <u>stroll **(1)**</u> through town!

- I'd rather be in my <u>bunk **(1)**</u> sleeping.

- A man has cuts on his <u>thigh **(1)**</u> and ankle.

- A large <u>fleet **(1)**</u> of fire trucks roars by.

- Large crevice in ground. Oak street is <u>split **(1)**</u> in two!

- It's hard to fully <u>grasp **(1)**</u> the power of a quake.

- Some people <u>claim **(1)**</u> that animals can predict earthquakes.

━━━ **Write a Safety Plan** On a separate sheet of paper, write about what you should do in an earthquake. Use the Spelling Review Words.

Responses will vary. **(5 points)**

Theme 1: **Nature's Fury**   73
Assessment Tip: Total **20** Points

Name _____

The Twister Is Right on Top of Us!

Write what kind of sentence each is—declarative, interrogative, imperative, or exclamatory.

1. The windows are breaking! <u>exclamatory **(1 point)**</u>

2. Cover your face with a towel. <u>imperative **(1)**</u>

3. We must stay together. <u>declarative **(1)**</u>

4. Has the tornado passed? <u>interrogative **(1)**</u>

Identify each sentence type. Then rewrite it as the type shown below.
Sample answers are shown.

5. You should help your brother. <u>declarative **(1)**</u>

   Imperative: <u>Help your brother. **(1)**</u>

6. The rain will stop soon. <u>declarative **(1)**</u>

   Interrogative: <u>Will the rain stop soon? **(1)**</u>

7. Does someone have a flashlight? <u>interrogative **(1)**</u>

   Declarative: <u>Someone has a flashlight. **(1)**</u>

8. The police are outside. <u>declarative **(1)**</u>

   Exclamatory: <u>The police are outside! **(1)**</u>

Assessment Tip: Total **12** Points

Name _____

Conjunction Functions

Circle each conjunction in the sentences below. Write *compound sentence* after each compound sentence.

1. A blanket of snow covered Manhattan (and) Brooklyn.
   (2 points) _____

2. The ice on the river looked thick, (but) no one walked out on it.
   compound sentence **(2)**

3. A boy put a ladder onto the ice (and) jumped up (and) down.
   (2) _____

4. The boy held the ladder, (and) people climbed down to the ice.
   compound sentence **(2)**

5. People stepped carefully onto the ice, (but) dogs ran onto it recklessly.
   compound sentence **(2)**

6. Were there more dogs (or) more people on the ice?
   (2) _____

Assessment Tip: Total **12** Points

Name _____

A Reporter's Tale

Use the words in the box to complete the news reporter's memo about Pecos Bill.

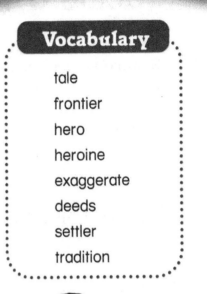

Vocabulary

tale
frontier
hero
heroine
exaggerate
deeds
settler
tradition

To: *The East Coast Gazette*

From: Gil Ibel, Gazette Staff

Subject: Pecos Bill Story

Last week I took a stagecoach to the Kansas frontier **(1 point)**_____. Since arriving, I have spoken to every settler **(1)**_____ in town, but have had no luck in getting an interview with Pecos Bill. However, I think I may have heard about every one of the amazing deeds **(1)**_____ he has ever done. It seems the folks around here have a tradition **(1)**_____ of gathering daily to swap Pecos Bill stories. He is unlike any other hero **(1)**_____ or heroine **(1)**_____ I have ever written about. At yesterday's meeting, I heard one tale **(1)**_____ about how Bill was raised by coyotes and another about how he came to use a rattlesnake as a whip. Then someone told me he'd left town on a cyclone headed for Arizona or Wyoming. I'm still not sure how to find him, but I do not exaggerate **(1)**_____ when I say that this is the best story I have ever followed!

Name _____

Tackle a Tall Tale

Tale _____

Sample answers are given.

Character, Setting, Plot
Main Character(s) Paul Bunyan **(2 points)**
Setting United States in the nineteenth century **(2)**
Plot: Important Events in the Tale Paul is born, outgrows his home, becomes a logger, cuts down forests across the country, builds the Big Onion Lumber Company. **(2)**

Tall Tale Exaggeration
Exaggerated Character Traits   Paul's growth as a baby; his appetite shown by his huge breakfast; his strength, felling "ten white pines with a single swing," and digging the Grand Canyon by dragging his pickaxe **(2)**
Exaggerated or Impossible Setting Elements a giant floating cradle off the coast of Maine; a mile-long bunkhouse **(2)**
Exaggerated or Impossible Actions or Events Paul causing an earthquake when he crawled as a baby; Paul digging ponds to provide drinking water; words freezing into icicles **(2)**
Factual Details locations in the United States; the growth of the lumber industry; loggers sleeping in the bunkhouse and eating together **(2)**

For me, the funniest part of this tall tale was Answers will vary. **(2)**

_____

Assessment Tip: Total **16** Points

Name _____

That Could Never Happen!

**Each of the four selections in *Focus on Tall Tales* contains at least
one exaggerated event. Write the event after each story title.**
Sample answers shown.

Paul Bunyan, the Mightiest Logger of Them All

Paul Bunyan chops down ten pine trees with one swing of his axe.

(2 points)

John Henry Races the Steam Drill

John Henry swings his hammer so hard and fast that it catches fire. **(2)**

Sally Ann Thunder Ann Whirlwind

Sally talks the grizzly bear into dancing with her, and at the same time

he churns her butter. **(2)**

February

McBroom saws chunks of the frozen wind during the winter and thaws

them out during the summer. **(2)**

Name _____

You'll Never Believe Whom I Just Met.

Think about characters you might find in a tall tale. Describe five tall tale characters by completing each sentence with an exaggeration. Sample answers shown.

1. This character is so tall that

   he has to duck whenever the space shuttle goes by. **(2 points)**

   _____

2. This character is so loud that

   when she clears her throat it causes an avalanche. **(2)**

   _____

3. This character is so old that

   he used to play hide-and-go-seek with the dinosaurs when he

   was a little boy. **(2)**

4. This character is so fast that

   she can run to the store, buy a quart of milk, and be back with

   the change before her father has finished writing *milk* on the

   shopping list. **(2)**

5. This character is so strong that

   when he loses something, he really does turn the house upside

   down to find it. **(2)**

Assessment Tip: Total **10** Points

Name _____

Tackle Another Tall Tale

Tale _____

Character, Setting, Plot
Main Character(s) Sally Ann Thunder Ann Whirlwind, Davy Crockett **(2 points)**
Setting United States in the nineteenth century **(2)**
Plot: Important Events in the Tale Davy Crockett is stuck in a tree; Sally rescues him; Davy falls in love with Sally and hears about her strength and cleverness; Davy proposes marriage and Sally accepts. **(2)**
Tall Tale Exaggeration
Exaggerated Character Traits Sally is super-strong (pulling on her rattlesnake rope), super-brave (riding a panther bareback) and can tame any animal (dancing with the King Bear). **(2)**
Exaggerated or Impossible Setting Elements trees bending and the wind blowing with the force of Davy hollering Sally's name **(2)**
Exaggerated or Impossible Actions or Events Sally bends the tree with a rattlesnake rope; she turns the dark to daylight with eye lightning; she knocks Mike Fink across the woods and into a swamp. **(2)**
Factual Details Davy Crockett; Maine to Louisiana; churning butter; foraging in the woods for berries **(2)**

Sample answers

For me, the funniest part of this tall tale was ___Answers will vary. **(2 points)**___

_____

Name _____

Growing Words from their Roots

Vis and *vid* are word roots. They have meaning, but are words by themselves. The Latin word roots *vis* and *vid* mean "to see."

television   videotape   supervision

Complete each sentence. Build a word containing the root *vis* or *vid*.

vis + ion	re + vis + e
e + vid + ent	pro + vid + e
vis + or	in + vis + ible

1. Max put on his <u>visor **(1 point)**</u> because the sun was in his eyes.

2. We missed the turn because the road sign was almost <u>invisible **(1)**</u> in the darkness.

3. When Hank slowly shuffled into class with his head down, it was <u>evident **(1)**</u> that he had not done his homework.

4. The factory has been without power for two days, but the new generator they bought will <u>provide **(1)**</u> enough energy.

5. The famous actor disliked the original script, so the writer was brought in to make a major <u>revision **(1)**</u>.

Now write sentences using four of the words you constructed.

<u>**(1 point** for each word)</u> _____

_____

_____

_____

Assessment Tip: Total **9** Points

Name _____

Long to Short

A long vowel sound may be spelled the same as a short vowel sound in words that are related in meaning.

     long vowel sound: divide

     short vowel sound: division

Write a pair of related Spelling Words in each row. Write each word under the heading that shows whether the common vowel letter or letters have a long or a short vowel sound. Underline the vowel letter or letters that are common in both words.
Order of word pairs may vary.

Spelling Words

1. steal
2. stealth
3. cave
4. cavity
5. wise
6. wisdom
7. deal
8. dealt
9. athlete
10. athletic
11. crime
12. criminal
13. breathe
14. breath
15. wild
16. wilderness
17. shade
18. shadow
19. revise
20. revision

Long Vowel Sound	Short Vowel Sound
steal **(1 point)**	stealth **(1)**
cave **(1)**	cavity **(1)**
wise **(1)**	wisdom **(1)**
deal **(1)**	dealt **(1)**
athlete **(1)**	athletic **(1)**
crime **(1)**	criminal **(1)**
breathe **(1)**	breath **(1)**
wild **(1)**	wilderness **(1)**
shade **(1)**	shadow **(1)**
revise **(1)**	revision **(1)**

Name _____

Spelling Spree

Letter Swap Write a Spelling Word by changing the underlined letter or letters to one or more different letters.

1. revi̱ve   revise **(1 point)**   6. wi̱fe   wise **(1)**
2. ḏeath   breath **(1)**   7. stea̱m   steal **(1)**
3. shap̱e   shade **(1)**   8. wav̱e   cave **(1)**
4. miḻd   wild **(1)**   9. mea̱l   deal **(1)**
5. shaḻlow   shadow **(1)**   10. wea̱lth   stealth **(1)**

Analogies An analogy compares word pairs that are related in the same way. An analogy might use pairs of opposites or pairs of synonyms, or it might show word pairs that name a category and an item in that category. Write the Spelling Word that completes each analogy.

> **Opposites:** *Hot* is to *cold* as *last* is to *first.*
> **Category and item:** *Hammer* is to *tool* as *peach* is to *fruit.*

11. *Building* is to *city* as *forest* is to wilderness **(1)**.
12. *Dentist* is to *doctor* as *burglar* is to criminal **(1)**.
13. *Sadness* is to *joy* as *foolishness* is to wisdom **(1)**.
14. *Iron* is to *rust* as *tooth* is to cavity **(1)**.
15. *Proofread* is to *correction* as *edit* is to revision **(1)**.

Spelling Words

1. steal
2. stealth
3. cave
4. cavity
5. wise
6. wisdom
7. deal
8. dealt
9. athlete
10. athletic
11. crime
12. criminal
13. breathe
14. breath
15. wild
16. wilderness
17. shade
18. shadow
19. revise
20. revision

Assessment Tip: Total **15 Points**

Name _____

Proofreading and Writing

Proofreading Circle the five misspelled Spelling Words in this paragraph from a tall tale. Then write each word correctly.
Order of answers may vary.

Back in the Old West, Burl Redwood was known far and wide as the most atheletic man who ever walked this planet. He could outrun, outjump, outride, outfight, outwrestle—just plain outdo anyone or anything. With great stealth Burl could sneak up on a grizzly bear, breeth down its neck, and then chase it for miles through the wilderness until the bear dropped from exhaustion. When Burl had a problem, he delt with it by holding a contest, which he always won.

One time, though, Burl committed a crim in a town policed by Wiley Wunn. That wise sheriff was eager to match wits with the famous athleet.

1. steal
2. stealth
3. cave
4. cavity
5. wise
6. wisdom
7. deal
8. dealt
9. athlete
10. athletic
11. crime
12. criminal
13. breathe
14. breath
15. wild
16. wilderness
17. shade
18. shadow
19. revise
20. revision

1. athletic **(1 point)**

2. breathe **(1)**

3. dealt **(1)**

4. crime **(1)**

5. athlete **(1)**

Make a Wanted Poster Think of a tall tale character whose special abilities might get him or her in trouble. Think about the character's abilities and what problems they might cause.

On a separate sheet of paper, create a wanted poster for your character. List the character's abilities and reasons why he or she is wanted. Use Spelling Words from the list. Responses will vary. **(5)**

Name _____

Informally Speaking

Tom has written a letter to Marissa, who lives in France. She doesn't know American slang very well and may not understand what Tom is talking about! Help make his letter easier to understand. Replace each underlined slang word or phrase with a proper word or phrase that means the same thing. Write the new word or words on the line that has the same number. Answers may vary. Sample answers are provided.

Dear Marissa,

 I'm <u>psyched</u> to come visit you this summer. Paris sounds so <u>cool</u>,
 ₁   ₂
and you're a real <u>pal</u> to invite me. My <u>old man</u> says he's been to France
 ₃   ₄
with my mom. He told me it's just as nice as it looks in the French <u>flicks</u>
 ₅
we rented at the video store. I've been watching a French-language show
on the <u>tube</u> so I can learn a few words and phrases. I figure if I <u>cram</u> for
 ₆   ₇
two weeks, I'll know how say hello and goodbye, and how to order some
of that famous French <u>chow</u>. I'm planning to <u>pig out</u> the whole time! If I
 ₈   ₉
<u>croak</u> after eating too many French pastries, <u>no sweat</u>!
 ₁₀   ₁₁
 Okay, I've got to hop on my <u>wheels</u> and deliver the local <u>rag</u> now,
 ₁₂   ₁₃
so I can earn some <u>greenbacks</u> for the trip. Talk to you soon!
 ₁₄

Your friend,

Tom

1. excited

2. good

3. friend

4. father

5. movies

6. television

7. study hard

8. food

9. eat a lot

10. die

11. no problem

12. bicycle/car

13. newspaper

14. money

Assessment Tip: Total **14** Points

Name _____

A Hairy Tale

Using Sentence Variety Use different types of sentences to make your writing more interesting and smooth to read. Use declarative, interrogative, imperative, or exclamatory sentences. Use compound sentences or sentences with compound subjects or compound predicates.

Rewrite these paragraphs describing a tall tale character. Change five sentences to introduce more sentence variety. **(2 points** for each sentence)

Maybe you have heard tales about Hairy Harry. Harry was born with long hair wrapped around him like a cocoon. His parents tied it in a ponytail. It dragged behind him like a king's robe for more than twenty feet.

Harry soon learned that he could use that hair like an extra arm. One time Harry fell down an old well. His sister, Harriet, fell in, too. Harry flipped his hair out of that well. He wrapped it around a tree trunk. Harriet climbed up his hair. Then Harry climbed up his hair. They were out of that well lickety-split.

Sample paragraphs. More than five changes are shown as examples.

Have you heard tales about Hairy Harry? Harry was born with long hair wrapped around him like a cocoon. His parents tied it in a ponytail, and it dragged behind him like a king's robe for more than twenty feet.

Harry soon learned that he could use that hair like an extra arm. One time Harry and his sister, Harriet, fell down an old well. Harry flipped his hair out of that well and wrapped it around a tree trunk. Harriet and Harry climbed up his hair and were out of that well lickety-split!

Name _____

Name a Noun

Appositives An appositive is a phrase that includes a noun that tells more about another noun in the same sentence. Use commas to set off an appositive.

Sally Ann Thunder Ann Whirlwind, <u>the title character</u>, was amazing.

Rewrite each sentence. Add the phrase from the box that tells more about the underlined noun. Use commas correctly.

| an alligator's skin |
| an eagle's nest |
| a muddy swamp |
| a riverboat man |
| his rival |

1. <u>Mike Fink</u> wanted to play a mean trick.

   Mike Fink, a riverboat man, wanted to play a mean trick. **(2 points)**

   _____

2. He was tired of hearing <u>Davy Crockett</u> praise Sally.

   He was tired of hearing Davy Crockett, his rival, praise Sally. **(2)**

   _____

3. Mike decided to wear a <u>disguise</u>.

   Mike decided to wear a disguise, an alligator's skin. **(2)**

   _____

4. Sally gave him a whack, and he landed in an uncomfortable <u>place</u>.

   Sally gave him a whack, and he landed in an uncomfortable place,

   a muddy swamp. **(2)**

5. Sally wore her favorite hat to meet Davy.

   Sally wore her favorite hat, an eagle's nest, to meet Davy. **(2)**

   _____

Assessment Tip: Total **10** Points

Name _____

Counselor Wanted

Using Commas with Appositives Use commas to set off an
appositive. If an appositive ends a sentence, it is followed by only
the end mark.

**Use proofreading marks to correct ten errors in punctuation
and capitalization in this job advertisement.**
(1 point for each correction)
Example: this job a real opportunity looks interesting

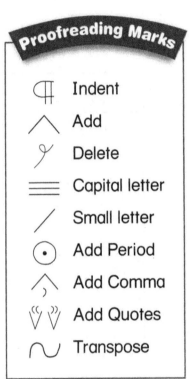

Proofreading Marks

⊞	Indent
∧	Add
૪	Delete
≡	Capital letter
/	Small letter
⊙	Add Period
∧	Add Comma
⌄⌄	Add Quotes
∿	Transpose

A great opportunity awaits you Camp
Timberlake a wilderness retreat for boys
and girls in Minnesota has an opening for
a junior counselor. Do you love the sound
of the wind and the smell of campfires?
Help our young campers children from
large cities learn about and appreciate the
sights, sounds, and smells of the outdoors.
Lead hikes and campfire songs tell and
create tall tales? We offer good pay and
plenty of fun. Apply at our office the first
red cabin.

Name _____

Planning a Tall Tale

Use the Chart to help plan your tall tale. (2 points each)

Character, Setting, Plot
Main Character(s)
Setting
Plot: Important Events in the Tale

Tall Tale Exaggeration
Exaggerated Character Traits
Exaggerated or Impossible Setting Elements
Exaggerated or Impossible Actions or Events
Realistic Details

Assessment Tip: Total **14** Points

Name _____

Using Exact Nouns

Choose an exact noun from the box to replace each underlined vague noun or noun phrase. Write your answers on the lines below.

Anna-Hanna-Diana was the most stunning gymnast in (1) <u>the continent</u>. When she jumped onto the balance beam, (2) <u>people</u> in the bleachers watched in awe. She did one (3) <u>thing</u> after another and then ended by turning somersaults as she leapt off. If you counted, you'd see she did (4) <u>lots</u> of them in midair.

One day Anna-Hanna-Diana heard that a big (5) <u>event</u> was going on in (6) <u>a state</u>. It started that very day. She said, "I'm going!"

Her mother said, "How will you get there? We're in New York! No (7) <u>transportation</u> can get you there quickly enough."

Well, Anna-Hanna-Diana got there on time. It took a fierce set of cross-country back flips to get her to (8) <u>that city</u> but she arrived in only a (9) <u>short time</u>. She won every (10) <u>item</u> at the meet, as usual.

1. North America **(1 point)**
2. fans **(1)**
3. cartwheel **(1)**
4. fifty-five **(1)**
5. gymnastics meet **(1)**
6. Arizona **(1)**
7. airplane **(1)**
8. Tucson **(1)**
9. half-hour **(1)**
10. trophy **(1)**

Exact Nouns

half-hour	fifty-five
Tucson	North America
airplane	fans
trophy	Arizona
cartwheel	gymnastics meet

92

Name _____

Give It All You've Got

How do the characters in this theme "give their all"? After reading each selection, answer the questions to complete the chart.

	Michelle Kwan: Heart of a Champion	La Bamba
What kind of writing is the selection an example of?	autobiography **(2.5 points)**	fiction **(2.5)**
What traits does the main character have? What actions or achievements help reveal those traits?	Michelle is aggressive, determined to succeed, and physically strong and agile. Her desire to be a Senior skater and her Olympic victory reveal these traits. **(2.5)**	Manuel is a show-off, but he is also funny and creative. His desire to be up on stage and his creative solution to the sticking record needle reveal these traits. **(2.5)**
Why does this selection belong in a theme called *Give It All You've Got*?	Michelle tried her best to become a great skater, an achievement that required much hard work. **(2.5)**	Manuel keeps on dancing when the needle sticks, even though he is embarrassed and feels like hiding. **(2.5)**
What advice might the main character give to others?	Reach high for your goals. Work hard and you can accomplish anything. **(2.5)**	Check your equipment before every performance. Think twice before you volunteer for a talent show. **(2.5)**

Assessment Tip: Total **10** points per selection and **2** points for the final question

Name _____

Give It All You've Got

	Mae Jemison: Space Scientist	The Fear Place
What kind of writing is the selection an example of?	biography **(2.5)**	fiction **(2.5)**
What traits does the main character have? What actions or achievements help reveal those traits?	Mae Jemison shows her intelligence through her educational achievements. She shows flexibility by changing careers. She shows artistic talent through dance, and leadership by forming a company. **(2.5)**	Doug is thoughtful and courageous. He forces himself to hike across a narrow ledge that terrifies him. He shows loyalty when he hikes alone to find his brother. **(2.5)**
Why does this selection belong in a theme called *Give It All You've Got*?	Mae Jemison succeeded at two very challenging careers, being a doctor and an astronaut. **(2.5)**	Doug hikes across the fear place even though it scares him. This takes great courage. **(2.5)**
What advice might the main character give to others?	Get a good education. Study what interests you and don't let others limit your goals or interests. **(2.5)**	Face your fear. **(2.5)**

What have you learned in this theme about facing challenges?

People can meet and overcome very difficult challenges if they find the strength and

courage within them. **(2)**

Assessment Tip: Total **10** points per selection and **2** points for the final question

Name _____

Top Marks

Read the word in each box from *Michelle Kwan: Heart of a Champion*. Write a word from the list that is related in meaning. Then use a dictionary to check if you were right.

pressure
stress **(1 point)**

required
specified **(1)**

presentations
demonstrations **(1)**

audience
spectators **(1)**

elements
components **(1)**

artistic
elegant **(1)**

judges
officials **(1)**

amateur
nonprofessional **(1)**

technical
skilled **(1)**

compete
perform **(1)**

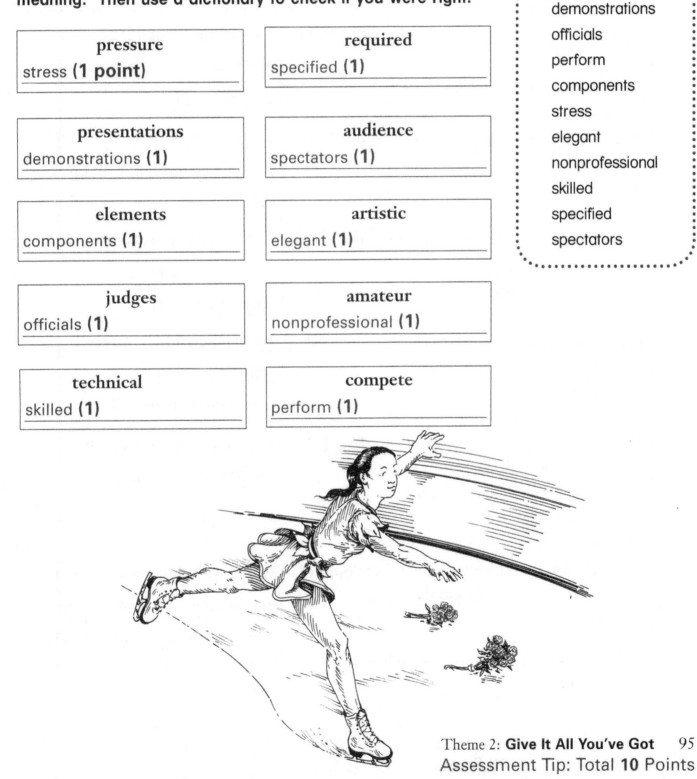

Name _____

Is That a Fact?

Passage	Fact or Opinion?	How I Can Tell
Page 139, paragraph 1: "I thought I was ready to become a Senior skater, at the age of twelve."	Opinion **(1)**	The words *I thought* are a clue that this is an opinion and cannot be proven. **(1)**
Page 140, paragraph 5: "Frank is one of the greatest coaches in the world."	Opinion **(1)**	The adjective *greatest* is a clue that this statement is an opinion. **(1)**
Page 144, paragraph 6: "The judges look for many required elements in a program."	Fact **(1)**	This fact could be proven by contacting the judging organization. **(1)**
Page 146, paragraph 3: "Elvis Stojko...does quadruple/triple combinations."	Fact **(1)**	This fact could be proven by watching a slow-motion videotape of Elvis. **(1)**
Page 147, paragraph 1: "Most elite skaters have three forty-five-minute-long practice sessions on the ice every day . . ."	Fact **(1)**	This fact could be proven by checking with all elite skaters. **(1)**
Page 150, paragraph 4: "And you can never forget how important school is."	Opinion **(1)**	This is Michelle's opinion—the words *how important* are clues that she is sharing a belief. **(1)**

Assessment Tip: Total **12** Points

Name _____

A Figure Skater's Trading Card

What if figure skaters were featured on trading cards as baseball players are? Complete the fact sheet so it gives vital information about Michelle Kwan. Then use the facts to write a paragraph that might appear on the back of a Michelle Kwan trading card.

FACT SHEET

Who Michelle Kwan is:

Ice skater **(1 point)**

Who her coach was:

Frank Carroll **(1)**

What she was especially good at when she was young:

She was a good jumper. **(1)**

Age at which she became a Senior skater:

12 years old **(1)**

How she had to improve in order to compete as a Senior skater:

Her skating had to become elegant and

she had to become a perfectionist in all

aspects. **(1)**

Her world records (see page 151):

Fifteen 6.0s for artistry **(1)**

Two pieces of advice she might give other young athletes:

1. Work hard. **(1)**

2. Be yourself. **(1)**

Michelle Kwan: Figure Skater

(4)

Name _____

Is That a Fact?

Read the following passage. Then answer the questions on page 99.

A Track Legend

Wilma Rudolph was perhaps the greatest female track athlete of her time. She was the first American woman to win three gold medals in a single Olympics. She also received many honors, including the Sullivan Award as the country's top amateur athlete, and a place in the Women's Sports Hall of Fame, the Black Sports Hall of Fame, and the United States Olympic Hall of Fame.

Rudolph achieved success despite great personal obstacles. As a child, she was stricken with polio, pneumonia, and scarlet fever. Some doctors said she would never walk. Yet no one could have been more determined to beat the odds. After years of physical therapy, Rudolph put aside her leg brace at age eleven and went on to become a great athlete in high school and college.

At the 1960 Olympic Games, Rudolph was the star of the American team. She won gold medals and set world records in the 100-meter dash, the 200-meter dash, and the 400-meter relay.

Rudolph later became a coach and a teacher. She also wrote a book about her life that was made into a movie. There has never been an American athlete who overcame more obstacles in life than Wilma Rudolph. She should be an inspiration to all Americans, and to athletes everywhere.

Name _____

Is That a Fact? continued

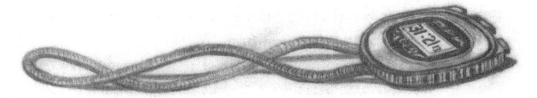

Answer these questions about the passage on page 98.

1. What opinion about Wilma Rudolph does the author give in the first paragraph? Write the sentence that states the opinion.
   Wilma Rudolph was perhaps the greatest female track athlete of her time.
   (2 points)

2. Which words in this sentence show that the statement is an opinion and not a fact?
   perhaps, greatest **(2)**

3. Which sentence from the second paragraph contains no opinions?
   As a child, she was stricken with polio, pneumonia, and scarlet fever. **(2)**

4. The third paragraph contains one opinion and several facts. Write them here.
   Opinion: Rudolph was the star of the American team at the 1960 Olympic Games. **(2)**

   Facts: She won gold medals and set world records in the 100-meter dash, the 200-meter dash, and 400-meter relay. **(4)**

5. Reread the last paragraph to find two facts and two opinions. Write them here.
   Opinion: Rudolph overcame more obstacles than any other American athlete. She should be an inspiration. **(4)**

   Facts: She became a coach and a teacher. She wrote a book about her life that was made into a movie. **(4)**

Name _____

Compound Creativity

Read the pairs of sentences. Identify the compound word in the first sentence, and write the words it is made from.

1. Even when my piano recital didn't go well, I believed in myself.

   my _____ + self **(1 point)** _____

2. Jen will do whatever it takes to make the soccer team.

   what _____ + ever **(1)** _____

3. Throughout the school year, I use the gym as often as I can.

   through _____ + out **(1)** _____

4. I have to do my homework before I can go biking with my friends.

   home _____ + work **(1)** _____

5. Philip spoke loudly from the stage so that everybody in the auditorium could hear him.

   every _____ + body **(1)** _____

Word Chain Play a compound word game. Start with a compound word. Use either of the words in it to form a new compound word. Then use part of the new word to form another compound. Keep your word chain going as long as you can. Sample answers shown.

Example: anymore ⟶ anyway ⟶ freeway ⟶ wayside ⟶ ?
sideline ⟶ outline ⟶ outboard ⟶ boardwalk ⟶ sidewalk
walkup ⟶ upstage ⟶ stagecoach ⟶ coachman **(5)**

Assessment Tip: Total **10** Points

Compound Words

A **compound word** is made up of two or more smaller words. To spell a compound word correctly, you must remember if it is written as one word, as a hyphenated word, or as separate words.

wheel + chair = wheelchair   **up + to + date** = up-to-date

first + aid = first aid

Write each Spelling Word under the heading that tells how the compound word is written. Order of answers for each category may vary.

Spelling Words

1. basketball
2. wheelchair
3. cheerleader
4. newscast
5. weekend
6. everybody
7. up-to-date
8. grandparent
9. first aid
10. wildlife
11. highway
12. daytime
13. whoever
14. test tube
15. turnpike
16. shipyard
17. homemade
18. household
19. salesperson
20. brother-in-law

One Word

basketball **(1 point)**

wheelchair **(1)**

cheerleader **(1)**

newscast **(1)**

weekend **(1)**

everybody **(1)**

grandparent **(1)**

wildlife **(1)**

highway **(1)**

daytime **(1)**

whoever **(1)**

turnpike **(1)**

shipyard **(1)**

homemade **(1)**

household **(1)**

salesperson **(1)**

With a Hyphen

up-to-date **(1)**

brother-in-law **(1)**

Separate Words

first aid **(1)**

test tube **(1)**

Theme 2: **Give It All You've Got**   101

Assessment Tip: Total **20** Points

Name _____

Spelling Spree

Exchanging Word Parts Write the Spelling Word that has one of the parts in each compound word below.

1. wildfire   wildlife **(1 point)**

2. dateline   up-to-date **(1)**

3. grandstand   grandparent **(1)**

4. sales tax   salesperson **(1)**

5. evergreen   whoever **(1)**

6. wayside   highway **(1)**

7. turnover   turnpike **(1)**

8. holdup   household **(1)**

Clue Addition Add the clues to create a Spelling Word.

9. large boat + play area =

10. comes before second + assist =

11. "Hooray!" + person in charge =

12. try out + hollow cylinder =

13. container made of twigs + sphere =

14. not night + what a watch measures =

15. circular frame with spokes + piece of furniture =

9. shipyard **(1)**

10. first aid **(1)**

11. cheerleader **(1)**

12. test tube **(1)**

13. basketball **(1)**

14. daytime **(1)**

15. wheelchair **(1)**

Assessment Tip: Total **15** Points

Name _____

Proofreading and Writing

Proofreading Circle the five misspelled Spelling Words in this transcript of a television news report. Then write each word correctly.

To end tonight's (newskast), we have a story about a local girl who made good. Debbie Martin, who started skating years ago on a pair of (homemad) skates, is going to the Junior Nationals. Debbie's parents, older sister, and (brother-in-lor) will accompany her to Seattle. For years, they have watched Debbie practice on the family's basketball court, which her father flooded in winter and allowed to freeze over. This (week-end) they will watch her in a world-class arena. We know that (everbody) in town will be rooting for Debbie!

1. newscast **(1 point)**

2. homemade **(1)**

3. brother-in-law **(1)**

4. weekend **(1)**

5. everybody **(1)**

Spelling Words

1. basketball
2. wheelchair
3. cheerleader
4. newscast
5. weekend
6. everybody
7. up-to-date
8. grandparent
9. first aid
10. wildlife
11. highway
12. daytime
13. whoever
14. test tube
15. turnpike
16. shipyard
17. homemade
18. household
19. salesperson
20. brother-in-law

Write a Comparison and Contrast Think of a sport you enjoy playing or watching. Does it have anything in common with figure skating? How is it different from figure skating?

On a separate piece of paper, write a paragraph in which you compare and contrast two sports. Use Spelling Words from the list. Responses will vary. **(5)**

Name _____

Word Family Matters

Decide which word best completes each sentence. Write the word in the blank.

1. When he realized that he had missed the team tryouts, Todd

   turned red with <u>fury **(1 point)**</u>   .

furious	fury	infuriate

2. Twenty school bands besides ours were entered in this year's

   state <u>competition **(1)**</u>   .

compete	competition	competitive

3. Vanilla ice cream with fudge sauce is a dessert I find

   <u>irresistible **(1)**</u>   .

irresistible	resistance	resist

4. Because the top math student receives a prize, my sister is

   <u>motivated **(1)**</u>   to get a good grade on her next test.

move	motion	motivated

5. Please wait <u>patiently **(1)**</u>   until it is your turn to play

   the computer game.

impatient	patience	patiently

Now write two sentences, using two words you have not used yet.
Sample answer shown.

6. <u>Waiting in line too long makes me impatient. **(2.5)**</u>

   _____

7. <u>I can't resist the sound of a parade. **(2.5)**</u>

   _____

Assessment Tip: Total **10** Points

Champion Michelle

Common and Proper Nouns A **common noun** names any person, place, or thing. A **proper noun** names a particular person, place, or thing. Each important word in a proper noun begins with a capital letter.

> We met at the **statue**. *statue:* common noun
> We met at the **Statue of Liberty**. *Statue of Liberty:* proper noun
> **Coach Boe** taught me how to skate. *Coach Boe:* proper noun
> A **coach** taught me how to skate. *coach:* common noun
> She is from another **state**. *state:* common noun
> She is from **California**. *California:* proper noun

Copy the nouns from the following sentences into the proper columns below. When you rewrite a proper noun, be sure to capitalize correctly.

1. debbie went to the skating rink on saturday.
2. In the winter, the pond is frozen.
3. miguel is fast when he puts on his skates.
4. I competed in the race at valley middle school.
5. Have you ever skated at rockefeller center?

Common Nouns	**Proper Nouns**
rink **(1 point)**	Debbie **(1)**
winter **(1)**	Saturday **(1)**
pond **(1)**	Miguel **(1)**
skates **(1)**	Valley Middle School **(1)**
race **(1)**	Rockefeller Center **(1)**

Assessment Tip: Total **10** Points

The People's Favorite

Singular and Possessive Nouns A **possessive noun** shows ownership or possession. To form a singular possessive noun, add an apostrophe and -*s* ('s). To form a plural possessive noun, add an apostrophe (') if the noun ends with *s*. Otherwise, add an apostrophe and -*s* ('s).

Singular	Singular Possessive	Plural	Plural Possessive
cat	cat's	cats	cats'
country	country's	countries	countries'
Jones	Jones's	Joneses	Joneses'
woman	woman's	women	women's
mouse	mouse's	mice	mice's

Fill in the blank in each sentence below with the possessive form of the noun in parentheses. Write an S on the line at the end of the sentence if you wrote a singular possessive noun. Write a P on the line if you wrote a plural possessive noun.

1. Our (school) _school's **(1 point)**_ skating club sponsored a citywide competition. _S_ **(1)**

2. The fifth grade (classes) _classes' **(1)**_ skaters were great. _P_ **(1)**

3. The first event was the (seniors) _seniors' **(1)**_ short program. _P_ **(1)**

4. The (competition) _competition's **(1)**_ rules were strict. _S_ **(1)**

5. The audience's favorite event was the (children) _children's **(1)**_ competition. _P_ **(1)**

Name _____

My Friend's Skating Pond

Writing Possessive Phrases It is easy to make a mistake when forming the possessive of a plural or a singular noun. Therefore, when you proofread, pay special attention to possessive nouns.

Chris in Maine wants to send this e-mail message to Joann in Florida. Proofread the message for errors in possessive nouns. Write the correct possessive forms above the line, as shown. (2 points for each word)

friends'
Example: My two friend's reports are about hockey.
              ^

To: joann@tropics.net
From: cwm@frozennorth.com
Re: Ice and Snow

Hi Joann!

                                        family's
    I have been ice-skating on my familys pond. The
                                          ^

pond froze solid last week. It is safe to skate on it
                    Tom's
now. Last evening, Toms family and my family skated
                        ^
                    families'
on the pond. Our families dogs played in the snow.
                        ^
        dogs'
The dogs tails never stopped wagging. They enjoyed
    ^
        winter's
this winters snow as much as we did!
        ^

                    Chris

Name _____

Writing an Announcement

How can you find out when and where Michelle Kwan is going to skate in a competition or perform in an exhibition? You might read an announcement on a bulletin board or in a newsletter, or you might hear one on the radio or TV. An **announcement** is a short speech or notice that gives important information about an event.

Fill in the chart below with details about an upcoming skating performance by Michelle Kwan or some other sporting event.

Date (3 points)
Time (3)
Place (3)
Cost (3)
Details about the program (3)

Now write your announcement on a separate sheet of paper. State the purpose of the announcement at the very beginning. Then provide information that answers these questions: *who? what? where? when? why? how?* **and** *how much?* **Be sure to include the exact date, time, location, and cost of the event as well as other details about the program. Use clear, interesting, and friendly language that the audience will understand. (5)**

Assessment Tip: Total **20** Points

Name _____

Ordering Important Information

A careful writer makes sure that the information in an announcement is complete and presented in a clear order. Sequence words, such as *first*, *next*, and *last*, help clarify the order of events and call attention to what is most important.

Somehow, this announcement has gotten scrambled. Reorder the sentences so that the announcement follows the sequence of events. Pay attention to sequence words that give clues to the order of the sentences. Then write the revised announcement on the lines below. (10 points)

After the match, a victory party will be held in the cafeteria. Game time is 3 P.M. Following the pep rally, the Bloomington Wildcats will play against the Forest Lane Eagles for the regional championship at O'Neill Field. During the rally, Coach Strauss will introduce all of the players and hand out free T-shirts and banners. There will be a pre-game pep rally tomorrow at 2:20 in the gym before the most important soccer match of the season. Go Wildcats!

There will be a pre-game pep rally tomorrow at 2:20 in the gym before the most important soccer match of the season. During the rally, Coach Strauss will introduce all of the players and hand out free T-shirts and banners. Following the pep rally, the Bloomington Wildcats will play against the Forest Lane Eagles for the regional championship at O'Neill Field. Game time is 3 P.M. After the match, a victory party will be held in the cafeteria. Go Wildcats!

Name _____

Revising Your Personal Essay

Reread your personal essay. Put a checkmark in the box for each sentence that describes your paper. Use this page to help you revise.

Rings the Bell

☐ I focused on one opinion and supported it with reasons and details.

☐ My reasons and details are organized in paragraphs.

☐ I wrote a strong introduction and a strong conclusion.

☐ I used precise words that make my feelings clear.

☐ Sentences flow smoothly. There are few mistakes.

Getting Stronger

☐ I focused on one opinion, but I need more reasons and details.

☐ My paragraphs are somewhat disorganized.

☐ My introduction and conclusion could be stronger.

☐ The words I chose don't always make my feelings clear.

☐ Some sentences are choppy. There are a few mistakes.

Try Harder

☐ I did not focus on one opinion. There are few reasons and details.

☐ My paper is just a list of thoughts.

☐ My introduction or conclusion are missing.

☐ Word choice is bland. My essay sounds flat.

☐ Most sentences are choppy. There are many mistakes.

Using Possessive Nouns

► Possessive nouns show ownership.
► To form the possessive of a singular noun add an apostrophe and *s*.
► To form the possessive case of a plural noun ending in *s*, add just an apostrophe.

**Rewrite each phrase, using a possessive noun. Then use the new
phrase in a sentence of your own.**

1. the music of the composer _the composer's music **(1)**_

   Sentences will vary.

2. the skill of the musicians _the musicians' skill **(1)**_

   Sentences will vary.

3. the authority of the conductor _the conductor's authority **(1)**_

   Sentences will vary.

4. the hush of the spectators _the spectators' hush **(1)**_

   Sentences will vary.

5. the sore throat of the actress _the actress's sore throat **(1)**_

   Sentences will vary.

6. the big chance for the understudy _the understudy's big chance **(1)**_

   Sentences will vary.

7. the groan of the audience _the audience's groan **(1)**_

   Sentences will vary.

8. the surprise of the critics _the critics' surprise **(1)**_

   Sentences will vary.

Name _____

Spelling Words

Look for familiar spelling patterns to help you remember how to spell the Spelling Words on this page. Think carefully about the parts that you find hard to spell in each word.

Write the missing letters in the Spelling Words below.

1. w <u>o</u> <u>u</u> <u>l</u> d **(1 point)**

2. w <u>o</u> <u>u</u> <u>l</u> dn't **(1)**

3. clo <u>t</u> <u>h</u> <u>e</u> <u>s</u> **(1)**

4. happ <u>e</u> <u>n</u> <u>e</u> <u>d</u> **(1)**

5. som <u>e</u> one **(1)**

6. sometim <u>e</u> <u>s</u> **(1)**

7. diff <u>e</u> r <u>e</u> nt **(1)**

8. an <u>o</u> ther **(1)**

9. w <u>e</u> i <u>r</u> d **(1)**

10. eig <u>h</u> t <u>h</u> **(1)**

11. c <u>o</u> <u>m</u> ing **(1)**

12. g <u>e</u> t t ing **(1)**

13. g <u>o</u> ing **(1)**

14. st <u>o</u> p p ed **(1)**

15. h <u>e</u> r <u>e</u> **(1)**

1. would
2. wouldn't
3. clothes
4. happened
5. someone
6. sometimes
7. different
8. another
9. weird
10. eighth
11. coming
12. getting
13. going
14. stopped
15. here

Study List On a separate piece of paper, write each Spelling Word. Check your spelling against the words on the list. Order of words may vary.

Assessment Tip: Total **15** Points

Name _____

Spelling Spree

Find a Rhyme **For each sentence write a Spelling Word that rhymes with the underlined word and makes sense in the sentence.**

1. The band _____ playing when the singer <u>dropped</u> his microphone.
2. When Alison <u>peered</u> out the window, she saw a _____ looking bird.
3. If my sweatshirt had a <u>hood</u>, I _____ definitely wear it on a day like this.
4. A <u>humming</u> sound was _____ from the car's engine.
5. We're _____ to the store after you finish <u>mowing</u> the lawn.
6. You <u>shouldn't</u> treat anyone in a way you _____ want to be treated yourself.
7. You have nothing to <u>fear</u> _____.

1. stopped **(1 point)**
2. weird **(1)**
3. would **(1)**
4. coming **(1)**
5. going **(1)**
6. wouldn't **(1)**
7. here **(1)**

Finding Words **Each word below is hidden in a Spelling Word. Write the Spelling Word.**

8. pen
9. on
10. eight
11. tin
12. cloth
13. not
14. met
15. rent

8. happened **(1)**
9. someone **(1)**
10. eighth **(1)**
11. getting **(1)**
12. clothes **(1)**
13. another **(1)**
14. sometimes **(1)**
15. different **(1)**

Spelling Words

1. would
2. wouldn't
3. clothes
4. happened
5. someone
6. sometimes
7. different
8. another
9. weird
10. eighth
11. coming
12. getting
13. going
14. stopped
15. here

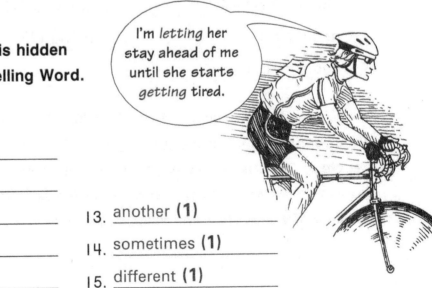

I'm *letting* her stay ahead of me until she starts *getting* tired.

Theme 2: **Give It All You've Got**   113
Assessment Tip: Total **15** Points

Name _____

Proofreading and Writing

Proofreading Circle the five misspelled Spelling Words in this certificate. Then write each word correctly.

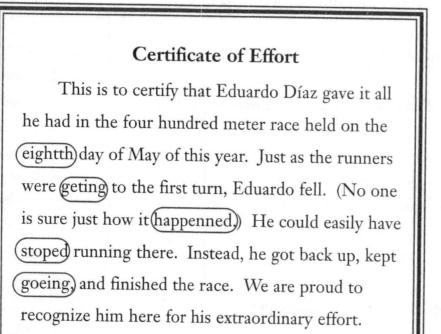

Certificate of Effort

This is to certify that Eduardo Díaz gave it all he had in the four hundred meter race held on the (eightth) day of May of this year. Just as the runners were (geting) to the first turn, Eduardo fell. (No one is sure just how it (happenned.)) He could easily have (stoped) running there. Instead, he got back up, kept (goeing,) and finished the race. We are proud to recognize him here for his extraordinary effort.

Spelling Words

1. would
2. wouldn't
3. clothes
4. happened
5. someone
6. sometimes
7. different
8. another
9. weird
10. eighth
11. coming
12. getting
13. going
14. stopped
15. here

1. eighth **(1 point)**
2. getting **(1)**
3. happened **(1)**
4. stopped **(1)**
5. going **(1)**

✏️ **Writing Headlines** Write four headlines for newspaper stories about people who gave it all they had. The headlines can be about people in the theme's selections, can be about people you know of from somewhere else, or can be completely made up. Include a Spelling Word in each headline. Responses will vary. **(5)**

Assessment Tip: Total **10** Points

Name _____

What a Performance!

Words are missing in the sentences. Fill each blank with a word or words from the box.

1. If you are the only one on stage, you are in the
   limelight **(1 point)** .

2. If you are good at something, you have
   talent **(1)** .

3. If you buy an old record with one song on each side, you
   become the owner of a forty-five record **(1)** .

4. If you have agreed to help, you have
   volunteered **(1)** .

5. If you act without speaking, you
   pantomime **(1)** .

6. If you perform for the first time, you make your
   debut **(1)** .

7. If you go to practice a play, you attend a
   rehearsal **(1)** .

8. If you forget your lines during a play, you may feel
   embarrassed **(1)** .

9. If you please the audience, you may hear
   applause **(1)** .

10. If you perform with a partner, you are part of a
    duo **(1)** .

Vocabulary

talent
pantomime
forty-five record
limelight
applause
volunteered
rehearsal
embarrassed
duo
debut

Assessment Tip: Total **10** Points

Name _____

Talent Report

Fill in the story map with information from the selection.

Characters	**Setting**
Manuel, Benny, Mr. Roybal,	Manuel's school and his home
Manuel's family **(2 points)**	**(2)**

Plot

Events

1. Manuel volunteers to be in the school talent show. He plans to pantomime the words to "La Bamba." **(2)**

2. Manuel practices his act at rehearsal. His forty-five record slips out of his hand and rolls across the floor. **(2)**

3. On the night of the talent show, all the kids who go onstage before Manuel do fine. **(2)**

4. Finally, it's Manuel's turn to perform. He is nervous when he steps onstage, but he starts to relax and have fun as his performance goes on and he hears the audience clapping. **(2)**

Problem

5. When Manuel is in the middle of his routine, the record skips. Manuel is embarrassed and doesn't know what to do. **(2)**

Solution

6. Manuel keeps repeating the same steps and mouthing the same line over and over. The audience loves the act and thinks Manuel made the record skip on purpose. **(2)**

Assessment Tip: Total **16** Points

Name _____

Manuel's Journal

Suppose Manuel wrote about the talent show in his journal. Finish each sentence to show what he might have said about his performance.

September _____, _____
                (today's date)   (year)

   I can't believe I survived the talent show. Here's how it happened. I'd volunteered to pretend to sing Ritchie Valens's "La Bamba" before the entire school. **(1 point)**. Two things happened at rehearsal that should have made me nervous. First, Mr. Roybal's record player speed jammed **(1)**. Then, when Benny blew his trumpet, I dropped the record **(1)**.

   On the night of the show, I had to wait for my turn onstage. A lot of other kids performed before me. As I watched them, I shivered with fear **(1)**. Finally it was my turn. At first, I took a dance step and the audience liked it and applauded. **(1)**. Then, suddenly, something awful happened: the record got stuck, and repeated the same line over and over **(1)**. I didn't know what to do, so I bowed to the audience, which applauded wildly **(1)**. As I left the stage, I tried hard to hold back the tears **(1)**.

   Here's the funny thing. After the performance I received a burst of applause that was so loud it shook the walls of the cafeteria **(1)**. I couldn't believe that people had actually liked my performance **(1)**.

Name _____

A Class Act

Read the story. Then complete the activity on page 119.

Horsing Around

Every year, the fifth grade classes held a big softball game and talent show. This year, Amy and Carmen decided to enter the talent show. Since their team was the Mustangs, the girls decided to dance in a horse costume. Amy would be the front half and Carmen the back half.

They spent an entire weekend making a papier-mâché horse's head. Carmen's dad sewed the body from fleecy brown cloth. The girls made the mane and tail out of thick black yarn. Amy's mom helped them learn a dance to a song called "Plains Pony."

At last it was the day of the show. But as the girls nervously galloped onto the softball diamond, they heard giggling from the audience. Someone called, "Hey, Horsey! You forgot something!" Carmen gasped, "Oh, no!" Peeking out from the horse's head, Amy saw something black near home plate. Their tail!

"What will we do?" Carmen whispered. Amy replied, "We'll pretend we planned it this way!" The next time they passed home plate, they danced around the tail and Amy snatched it up. Then she and Carmen danced backwards off the field, shaking their hooves to the music as Amy waved goodbye with the tail. The audience applauded noisily, screaming with laughter.

Name _____

A Class Act continued

Fill in the story map so it sums up the story on page 118. Write the characters' names, the setting, and the events that make up the plot.

Main Characters	Setting (time and place)
Amy and Carmen **(1 point)**	a school in modern times **(1)**

Plot

The fifth graders hold an annual softball game and talent show. Amy and Carmen decide to dance in the show as a horse. They work hard on a costume. The girls face a problem during the show — their tail falls off. Through quick thinking, they solve their problem and are a success. **(4)**

Problem

As they go out onto the field to start their dance, their horse's tail falls off. The girls are embarrassed. **(2)**

Solution

Amy tells Carmen to pretend that they planned to drop the tail. They pick it up and use it to wave goodbye to the audience. The audience loves it. **(2)**

Record Roots

Some words in the box contain the word root *spec*.
Others contain the root *opt*. Write the words that match each
clue. Then write each numbered letter in the space with the
matching number to find a message.

inspector
optician
optometry
respect
spectacle
suspect

1. a person who makes or sells eyeglasses

    <u>o</u> <u>p</u> <u>t</u> <u>i</u> <u>c</u> <u>i</u> <u>a</u> <u>n</u> **(1 point)**
       9   6

2. to look up to or regard highly

    <u>r</u> <u>e</u> <u>s</u> <u>p</u> <u>e</u> <u>c</u> <u>t</u> **(1)**
    7

3. a remarkable or impressive sight

    <u>s</u> <u>p</u> <u>e</u> <u>c</u> <u>t</u> <u>a</u> <u>c</u> <u>l</u> <u>e</u> **(1)**
       3   5

4. the profession of examining a person's vision

    <u>o</u> <u>p</u> <u>t</u> <u>o</u> <u>m</u> <u>e</u> <u>t</u> <u>r</u> <u>y</u> **(1)**
                       10

5. to look upon someone as guilty without proof

    <u>s</u> <u>u</u> <u>s</u> <u>p</u> <u>e</u> <u>c</u> <u>t</u> **(1)**
       4   1

6. a person who examines something closely and carefully

    <u>i</u> <u>n</u> <u>s</u> <u>p</u> <u>e</u> <u>c</u> <u>t</u> <u>o</u> <u>r</u> **(1)**
     8   2

Manuel gained a lot of <u>p</u> <u>o</u> <u>p</u> <u>u</u> <u>l</u> <u>a</u> <u>r</u> <u>i</u> <u>t</u> <u>y</u> after
his performance.   1 2 3 4 5 6 7 8 9 10
(4 points)

Assessment Tip: Total **10** Points

Name _____

The /ou/, /ô/, and /oi/ Sounds

When you hear the /ou/, the /ô/, and the /oi/ sounds, think of these patterns:

/ou/ *ou, ow* **ou**nce, t**ow**er

/ô/ *aw, au, a* before *l* cl**aw**, p**au**se, b**a**ld

/oi/ *oi, oy* m**oi**st, l**oy**al

Remember that the patterns *ou*, *au*, and *oi* are usually followed by a consonant sound.

Write each Spelling Word under its vowel sound.
Order of answers for each category may vary.

Spelling Words

1. hawk
2. claw
3. bald
4. tower
5. halt
6. prowl
7. loyal
8. pause
9. moist
10. ounce
11. launch
12. royal
13. scowl
14. haunt
15. noisy
16. coward
17. fawn
18. thousand
19. drown
20. fault

/ou/ Sound

tower **(1 point)**

prowl **(1)**

ounce **(1)**

scowl **(1)**

coward **(1)**

thousand **(1)**

drown **(1)**

/ô/ Sound

hawk **(1)**

claw **(1)**

bald **(1)**

halt **(1)**

pause **(1)**

launch **(1)**

haunt **(1)**

fawn **(1)**

fault **(1)**

/oi/ Sound

loyal **(1)**

moist **(1)**

royal **(1)**

noisy **(1)**

Name _____

Spelling Spree

Contrast Clues The second part of each clue contrasts with the first part. Write a Spelling Word after each clue.

1. not hairy, but <u>bald</u> **(1 point)**

2. not a traitor, but <u>loyal</u> **(1)**

3. not a smile, but a <u>scowl</u> **(1)**

4. not to dock, but to <u>launch</u> **(1)**

5. not an adult deer, but a <u>fawn</u> **(1)**

6. not a pound, but an <u>ounce</u> **(1)**

7. not a sparrow, but a <u>hawk</u> **(1)**

8. not lowly or common, but <u>royal</u> **(1)**

9. not quiet, but <u>noisy</u> **(1)**

10. not to move about openly, but to <u>prowl</u> **(1)**

Finding Words Each word below is hidden in a Spelling Word. Write the Spelling Words that contain these words.

11. aunt <u>haunt</u> **(1)**

12. tow <u>tower</u> **(1)**

13. sand <u>thousand</u> **(1)**

14. law <u>claw</u> **(1)**

15. use <u>pause</u> **(1)**

Spelling Words

1. hawk
2. claw
3. bald
4. tower
5. halt
6. prowl
7. loyal
8. pause
9. moist
10. ounce
11. launch
12. royal
13. scowl
14. haunt
15. noisy
16. coward
17. fawn
18. thousand
19. drown
20. fault

Assessment Tip: Total **15** Points

Name _____

Proofreading and Writing

Circle the five misspelled Spelling Words in this e-mail that Manuel might have sent. Then write each word correctly.

File	Edit	View	Toolbox	Help	✉

To: Grandma

From: Manuel

Subject: Talent Show

   The show turned out okay, but I was pretty nervous beforehand. My hands were (moyst) with sweat. I'm no (cowerd,) though. I went out and started my act. Then the record stuck, and I had to sing the same words over and over. It was Benny's (falt) for making me scratch the record. When the music finally came to a (hault,) I ran offstage. I felt awful! At the end of the show, though, I got a round of applause noisy enough to (droun) out the names of the other acts. Nobody was more surprised than I was!

1. moist **(1 point)**

2. coward **(1)**

3. fault **(1)**

4. halt **(1)**

5. drown **(1)**

Spelling Words

1. hawk
2. claw
3. bald
4. tower
5. halt
6. prowl
7. loyal
8. pause
9. moist
10. ounce
11. launch
12. royal
13. scowl
14. haunt
15. noisy
16. coward
17. fawn
18. thousand
19. drown
20. fault

✏ **Write an Announcement** Suppose that Manuel decided to give another performance of "La Bamba." How would you go about advertising it? What information would you need to include? How would you describe his act?

On a separate piece of paper, write an announcement for this repeat performance. Use Spelling Words from the list. Responses will vary. **(5)**

Name _____

Mixed Meanings

**Read the definitions of each word. Then write one or two sentences
that use different meanings of each word.** Sample answers shown.

fall (fôl) *v.* **fell, fallen, falling, falls. 1.** To drop or come down. **2.** To suffer
defeat or capture. **3.** *n.* The season of the year occurring between summer
and winter.

1. During the fall, I love to watch leaves fall from the

   trees to the ground. **(2 points)**

hand (hănd) *n.* **1.** The part of the arm below the wrist. **2.** A round of applause.
v. To give or pass with the hands; transmit.

2. The director handed Bonnie a bouquet of flowers as the audienc

   gave her a hand. **(2)**

stage (stāj) *n.* **1.** A raised platform, especially one in a theater on which
entertainers perform. **2.** A level or step in a process. *v.* To produce or
direct a performance.

3. Sheila's school stages a musical every spring. My mother says my

   baby brother is at a difficult stage. **(2)**

step (stĕp) *n.* **1.** The movement of raising one foot and putting it down. **2.** An
action taken to achieve a goal. *v.* To press the foot down or against.

4. If you follow the steps correctly, you'll make a perfect kite. Every

   step I take brings me a little closer to the campground. **(2)**

stick (stĭk) *n.* A long slender piece of wood. *v.* **1.** To fasten or attach, as with a
pin or nail. **2.** To become fixed and unable to move.

5. Freddy's dog likes to chase sticks. Peanut butter sticks to the roof

   of my mouth. **(2)**

Assessment Tip: Total **10** Points

Name _____

Mary Sings and Puppets Move

Action Verbs An **action verb** tells what the subject does or did. It is the main word in the complete predicate.

The performers **bowed** to the audience.
action verb

Underline the action verb in each of the following sentences. (1 point each)

1. Martin and Mary <u>built</u> a small theater for their puppet show.

2. Martin's father <u>cut</u> the wood for them.

3. Martin <u>painted</u> designs on the wooden theater.

4. Mary <u>picked</u> a song for their show.

5. On the night of the show, Martin <u>watches</u> the audience.

6. The audience <u>claps</u> for the tap dancer.

7. Martin and Mary <u>carry</u> their puppets on stage.

8. The puppets <u>dance</u> to the music.

9. The puppeteers <u>wait</u> for applause.

10. The crowd <u>cheers</u>!

Name _____

He Gave a Speech

Direct Objects A **direct object** is a noun or pronoun in a predicate that receives the action of the verb. It answers the question *What?* or *Whom?*

> The dancer tied his **shoes.**
>
> The dancer tied *what?* His shoes. Therefore, *shoes* is the direct object.

Underline the action verb and circle the direct object in each sentence below.

1. Mr. Bruno <u>needed</u> a (volunteer) to give a speech. **(1 point)**

2. Sydney <u>raised</u> his (hand.) **(1)**

3. Mr. Bruno <u>thanked</u> (him) for volunteering. **(1)**

4. Sydney nervously <u>shuffled</u> his (notes.) **(1)**

5. Then he <u>cleared</u> his (throat.) **(1)**

6. He <u>projected</u> his (voice) throughout the room. **(1)**

7. Susan <u>heard</u> his (words) in the back of the classroom. **(1)**

8. After the speech, Mario <u>asked</u> a (question) of Sydney. **(1)**

9. Sydney <u>answered</u> the (query) politely. **(1)**

10. Then Sydney <u>set</u> his (notes) down. **(1)**

Assessment Tip: Total **10** Points

Name _____

She Wrote and I Scribbled

Using Exact Verbs Your writing will be more vivid if you use action verbs that tell exactly what the subject of the sentence is doing. Look at the two sentences below. Which verb gives you a better idea of how Sandy made her way across the stage?

> Sandy **moved** across the stage.
> Sandy **twirled** across the stage.

Pat is writing a review of the class play for the school newspaper. Replace each underlined verb with a more exact one. Choose from among the verbs in the box. Answers may vary. **(1 point for each word)**

stomped
stumbled
shouted
fumbled
scribbled

Last night I saw the class play *Ramshackle Inn*. There were five main

characters. The innkeeper was a loud man with a beard. When he said his   *shouted*

lines, others onstage covered their ears. The brother was clumsy. He

stumbled   *stomped*
walked back and forth across the stage. His rude and angry sister walked

scribbled
up and down the stairs. The reporter wrote constantly in his pad. The

fumbled
inept police officer was the funniest character of all. She played with her

radio, trying to get it to work. The plot of this play was silly, but the

actors were fun to watch.

Name _____

Writing a Summary

If you were asked to summarize "La Bamba," you would probably tell who performed in the talent show and what happened during the performances. A **summary** is a brief account of a story or selection. Writing a summary is a good way to share what a story is about and to recall main events and characters.

Choose a selection you have read, such as *Earthquake Terror* or *Michelle Kwan: Heart of a Champion*. Then fill in the graphic organizer below with the most important ideas or events in the selection.

Selection: _____

Idea/ Event	Idea/ Event	Idea/ Event	Idea/ Event
(3 points)	(3)	(3)	(3)

Now write your summary of the selection on a separate sheet of paper. Remember to leave out details and minor events. Briefly restate the most important ideas or events in your own words. (3)

Assessment Tip: Total **15** Points

Name _____

Paraphrasing

When you **paraphrase** a passage from a book, article, or story, you put it into your own words without changing the author's meaning. A careful writer makes sure to paraphrase without copying any passages word-for-word from the work of other writers.

Read the following passage from "La Bamba."

> But when Manuel did a fancy dance step, there was a burst of applause and some girls screamed. Manuel tried another dance step. He heard more applause and screams and started getting into the groove as he shivered and snaked around the stage. But the record got stuck, and he had to sing
>
> *Para bailar la bamba*
> *Para bailar la bamba*
> *Para bailar la bamba*
> *Para bailar la bamba*
> again and again.

Now read one fifth grader's paraphrase of the passage.

Paraphrase

Manuel did one fancy dance step and then another. The audience applauded and screamed when he shivered and snaked across the stage. Then the record got stuck, and he sang one line of "La Bamba" again and again.

Improve the student's paraphrase by reducing it to a single sentence that tells what happened in the passage. You may want to reorder the information and reduce the number of details. Be sure to avoid repetition of whole phrases that appeared in the original passage. Write your improved version on the lines below. Responses will vary. **(10 points)**

Even though Manuel was forced to lip-synch one line repeatedly when his record

got stuck, the audience responded enthusiastically to his pantomime of "La Bamba."

Name _____

Have No Fear

Read the words in the chart. Then look in the word box to find a synonym and an antonym for each, and write these in the chart. Use a dictionary if you need help.

	synonym	antonym
terrified	frightened **(1)**	unafraid **(1)**
dismayed	bewildered **(1)**	untroubled **(1)**
excitement	agitation **(1)**	monotony **(1)**
stamina	strength **(1)**	weakness **(1)**
concentrate	focus **(1)**	disregard **(1)**
discomfort	pain **(1)**	comfort **(1)**
unsure	uncertain **(1)**	sure **(1)**
cautious	careful **(1)**	reckless **(1)**
immobile	stationary **(1)**	mobile **(1)**

Choose a word from the word box and write your own sentence.

(2) _____

_____

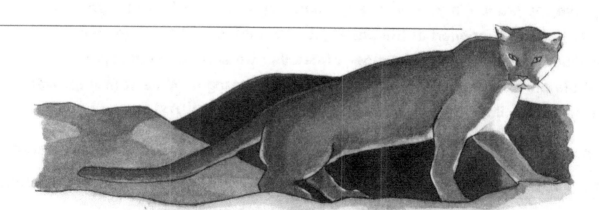

Assessment Tip: Total **20** Points

Name _____

I Predict . . .

Fill in the chart with your predictions, based on details from the selection and on what you know from personal experience.

Predicting Outcomes
selection details + personal knowledge + THINKING = prediction

Selection Details	Personal Knowledge
► Doug needs to get past a narrow ledge.	► People who have done something before, even if it was difficult, know that they can do it again.
► The journey seems futile.	
► Doug has made it to the narrow ledge before.	

Prediction: Doug will make it back to the ledge.

Selection Details (2 points)	Personal Knowledge (2)
_____ _____	_____ _____

Prediction: (1) _____

_____

Selection Details (2 points)	Personal Knowledge (2)
_____ _____	_____ _____

Prediction: (1) _____

_____

Name _____

Events Leading to the Climax

The events in *The Fear Place* lead to a climax when Doug must face his fear. Fill in the event map with sentences that describe the events that lead up to and come after the climax. Start at the bottom of the page.

7. Doug knows he is past the "fear place" when he comes to a part of the path that is wider and safer. **(2)**

↑

6. When Doug reaches the narrowest part of the ledge, he edges his way across it carefully. **(2)**

↑

5. Doug reaches the "fear place" and slowly begins to move across the ledge. **(2)**

↑

4. Doug watches where Charlie goes and follows her up the path as it gets narrower and narrower. **(2)**

↑

3. Charlie appears on the scene and startles Doug. **(2)**

↑

2. Doug reaches the first ridge. He thinks about the weather to keep his mind off of his fear. **(2)**

↑

1. Doug begins to climb, but every time he gains altitude he loses it again. **(2)**

Assessment Tip: Total **14** Points

Name _____

Looking Forward

Read the passage. Then complete the activity on page 134.

The Apology

Alexa hadn't meant to break the bowl. In fact, she'd always loved that china bowl and its pretty blue pattern. But she had broken it, and all week she'd listened with dread for the phone call she knew would come. It would be Mrs. Holabird, their neighbor, calling to tell her mother about the accident.

The Holabirds had no children of their own, so they were especially fond of Alexa. She had been helping Mrs. Holabird with chores for about two years. When they went out of town, the Holabirds always paid Alexa to cat-sit for Misty. Alexa would come twice a day and refill Misty's food and water bowls. She usually stayed for a while, holding the big, silky cat on her lap and scratching her behind the ears. Sometimes she helped Misty exercise. It was fun to toss a ball or a catnip mouse into the air and watch the fat, fluffy cat leap and grab for it with her paws. How was she to know that Misty would crash into the bowl and knock it off its stand?

Alexa had been so horrified that she had hidden the broken pieces under the sideboard. She went home and fearfully awaited the phone call. But three days later it still had not come, even though the Holabirds had returned two days ago.

On the fourth morning, Alexa awoke with her mind made up. She put on her coat and walked to the front door, calling, "Mom, I need to go see Mr. and Mrs. Holabird."

Name _____

Looking Forward continued

Answer these questions about the passage on page 133.

1. What do you think Alexa will do next?
   <u>She will go over to the Holabirds' house, tell them about the</u>
   <u>accident, and apologize.</u> **(2 points)**

2. What clues in the passage helped you make this prediction?
   <u>The first three paragraphs make clear that Alexa feels sorry about</u>
   <u>breaking the bowl and is afraid that Mrs. Holabird will call her</u>
   <u>mother. The fourth paragraph says that Alexa awoke with her mind</u>
   <u>made up and told her mother she needed to see the Holabirds.</u> **(4)**

3. Do you think Alexa's mother will be glad that Alexa apologized to
   Mrs. Holabird? Why or why not?
   <u>Yes, because that is what parents usually want their children to do</u>
   <u>if they have done something wrong.</u> **(2)**

4. Do you think the Holabirds will ask Alexa to care for Misty again?
   Why or why not?
   <u>Yes, because they are especially fond of Alexa and she has helped</u>
   <u>them with chores for two years.</u> **(2)**

5. What might Alexa do to make up for breaking the bowl?
   <u>She might offer to pay for it or to work off its value by doing</u>
   <u>chores.</u> **(2)**

6. What is one thing Alexa might do differently the next time she plays
   with Misty?
   <u>She might make sure to play with her outside or in a room that</u>
   <u>doesn't have breakable objects.</u> **(2)**

134   Theme 2: **Give It All You've Got**
Assessment Tip: Total **14** Points

Name _____

Nervous? No, Onward!

Read this diary page. Underline each word with the suffix *-ward* or *-ous*. (1 point for each underlined word)

The Hike

Climbing to the mountaintop was a frightening experience. At first, it didn't seem so bad. The path <u>upward</u> was wide, even <u>spacious</u>. After a while, though, I began to be <u>nervous</u>. The rise was <u>continuous</u>, and the path began to narrow. When I looked over the edge, I saw a <u>monstrous</u> gap between me and the canyon bottom far below. Still, I made my way <u>toward</u> the top, pausing only now and then. I knew that if I glanced <u>backward</u>, I would be in trouble. Instead, I gazed <u>outward</u> to the golden plain in the distance. It was a <u>marvelous</u> sight. I knew I would head <u>homeward</u> in less than an hour.

Now write each word you underlined next to its meaning.

1. toward **(1 point)** _____ : in a direction nearer
2. nervous **(1)** _____ : uncomfortable
3. outward **(1)** _____ : in a direction away from
4. monstrous **(1)** _____ : huge
5. homeward **(1)** _____ : toward where one lives
6. upward **(1)** _____ : heading above
7. backward **(1)** _____ : to the rear
8. spacious **(1)** _____ : roomy
9. continuous **(1)** _____ : ongoing, with no break
10. marvelous **(1)** _____ : wonderful

Name _____

The /ôr/, /âr/, and /är/ Sounds

When you hear the /ôr/ sound, think of the patterns *or*, *oar*, and *ore*. When you hear the /âr/ sound, think of the patterns *are* and *air*. When you hear the /är/ sound, think of the pattern *ar*.

> /ôr/ t**or**ch, s**oar**, s**ore**   /âr/ h**are**, fl**air**   /är/ sc**ar**

▶ The vowel sound + *r* spellings of the starred words differ from the usual spelling patterns. The /ôr/ sound is spelled *ar* in *warn* and *oor* in *floor*.

Write each Spelling Word under its vowel + r sound.
Order of answers for each category may vary.

Spelling Words
1. hare
2. scar
3. torch
4. soar
5. harsh
6. sore
7. lord
8. flair
9. warn*
10. floor*
11. tore
12. lair
13. snare
14. carve
15. bore
16. fare
17. gorge
18. barge
19. flare
20. rare

/ôr/ Sound

torch **(1 point)**

soar **(1)**

sore **(1)**

lord **(1)**

warn **(1)**

floor **(1)**

tore **(1)**

bore **(1)**

gorge **(1)**

/âr/ Sound

hare **(1)**

flair **(1)**

lair **(1)**

snare **(1)**

fare **(1)**

flare **(1)**

rare **(1)**

/är/ Sound

scar **(1)**

harsh **(1)**

carve **(1)**

barge **(1)**

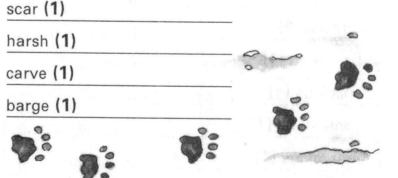

Assessment Tip: Total **20** Points

Name _____

Spelling Spree

Word Hunt Write the Spelling Word that you find in each of the longer words below.

Example: snowboarder *board*

1. torchlight   <u>torch **(1 point)**</u>

2. harebrained   <u>hare **(1)**</u>

3. warlord   <u>lord **(1)**</u>

4. scarcely   <u>scar **(1)**</u>

5. welfare   <u>fare **(1)**</u>

6. restored   <u>tore **(1)**</u>

7. floorshow   <u>floor **(1)**</u>

Alphabet Puzzler Write the Spelling Word that fits alphabetically between the two words in each group.

8. apple, <u>barge **(1)**</u>, bicycle

9. butter, <u>carve **(1)**</u>, dinner

10. ladder, <u>lair **(1)**</u>, loan

11. sock, <u>sore **(1)**</u>, stomach

12. father, <u>flair **(1)**</u>, flame

13. harmful, <u>harsh **(1)**</u>, kitchen

14. sneeze, <u>soar **(1)**</u>, solid

15. secret, <u>snare **(1)**</u>, snow

Spelling Words

1. hare
2. scar
3. torch
4. soar
5. harsh
6. sore
7. lord
8. flair
9. warn*
10. floor*
11. tore
12. lair
13. snare
14. carve
15. bore
16. fare
17. gorge
18. barge
19. flare
20. rare

Proofreading and Writing

Proofreading Circle the five misspelled Spelling Words in this part of a note. Then write each word correctly.

To the Park Rangers:

I have to leave unexpectedly for a day. Will you keep an eye on my two boys, who are camping on the north ledge? They are experienced climbers, but their tempers sometimes (flar) when they're alone with each other. For that matter, it's (rair) for them to get along anytime! The younger one has a sore knee from sliding down a (gorg.) I won't (boar) you with the details, but I would appreciate it if you could check on them during the day. I'll (woarn) them to behave themselves.

1. flare **(1 point)**
2. rare **(1)**
3. gorge **(1)**
4. bore **(1)**
5. warn **(1)**

Spelling Words

1. hare
2. scar
3. torch
4. soar
5. harsh
6. sore
7. lord
8. flair
9. warn*
10. floor*
11. tore
12. lair
13. snare
14. carve
15. bore
16. fare
17. gorge
18. barge
19. flare
20. rare

Write a Prediction Now that Doug has made it past the Fear Place, what do you think will happen next? Will he find his brother safe or in danger? Will Charlie continue to help him?

On a separate piece of paper, write a paragraph giving your prediction of what will happen next in the story. Use Spelling Words from the list. Responses will vary. **(5)**

Assessment Tip: Total **10** Points

Name _____

Homophone Echoes

Match the letter of the correct definition to the underlined word. Then write the homophone pairs at the bottom of the page. (1 point each)

1. The hiker makes her way through a narrow canyon. __a__

2. As she climbs, objects below <u>seem</u> to get smaller __e__

3. She kneels beside the <u>burrow</u> of a ground squirrel. __f__

4. In the distance she can see a snow-capped <u>peak</u>. __h__

5. Will she <u>freeze</u> when she gets to the top? __i__

6. She takes a quick <u>peek</u> into the canyon. __c__

7. The <u>seam</u> in her boot rubs her heel. __d__

8. She's a long way from the <u>borough</u> of Brooklyn! __j__

9. If she <u>threw</u> a stone, it might cause a rockslide below. __b__

10. Watching an eagle fly <u>frees</u> her from her fear. __g__

a. in and out of
b. tossed
c. glance
d. stitch
e. appear
f. tunnel
g. liberates
h. summit
i. be cold
j. city section

11. __through__   __threw__

12. __peek__   __peak__

13. __seam__   __seem__

14. __freeze__   __frees__

15. __burrow__   __burough__

Name _____

We Are Diving

Main Verbs and Helping Verbs A simple predicate can be more than one word. The **main verb** is the most important word in the predicate. The **helping verb** comes before the **main verb**.

I **have climbed** the rope.   main verb: *climbed*   helping verb: *have*

Write the main verb and the helping verb in each of the following sentences.

1. This summer camp program has challenged me.

Main verb: challenged **(1 point)**

Helping verb: has **(1)**

2. I am facing my fear of water in the swimming classes.

Main verb: facing **(1)**

Helping verb: am **(1)**

3. The swimming teacher has given me much encouragement.

Main verb: given **(1)**

Helping verb: has **(1)**

4. I have swum two laps so far this morning.

Main verb: swum **(1)**

Helping verb: have **(1)**

5. Next summer, I will learn to dive!

Main verb: learn **(1)**

Helping verb: will **(1)**

Assessment Tip: Total **10** Points

Name _____

Jellyfish Are Nasty

Linking Verbs A **linking verb** links the subject to a word in the predicate that names or describes the subject. It does not show action. A **predicate noun** following a linking verb names the subject. A **predicate adjective** following a linking verb describes the subject.

Common Linking Verbs

am	is	are	was	were	will be
look	feel	taste	smell	seem	appear

Underline the linking verb in each sentence below. Circle each predicate noun or predicate adjective. Write *PN* on the line if the circled word is a predicate noun. Write *PA* if it is a predicate adjective. (1 point for each)

Example: I <u>am</u> a (swimmer.) __PN__

1. Susan <u>will be</u> a (lifeguard) someday. __PN__
2. Lifeguards <u>are</u> (brave.) __PA__
3. The ocean breeze <u>smells</u> (fresh.) __PA__
4. I <u>am</u> (afraid) of jellyfish. __PA__
5. A sea nettle <u>is</u> a (jellyfish.) __PN__
6. Ocean water <u>tastes</u> (salty.) __PA__
7. That boat <u>is</u> a (kayak.) __PN__
8. My grandmother <u>was</u> a (diver.) __PN__
9. That stroke <u>seems</u> (difficult) to me. __PA__
10. Clayton and Rachel <u>are</u> (surfers.) __PN__

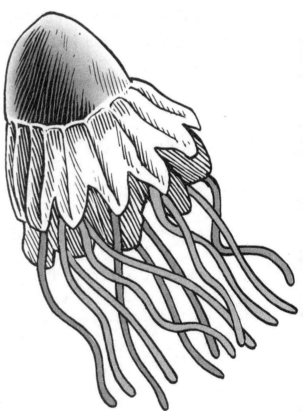

Name _____

Are You Afraid?

Using Forms of the Verb *be* When using *be* as a linking verb, a writer must use the correct form of the verb. Like any other verb, a linking verb must agree with its subject in number.

	The Verb *be*	
	Present Tense	**Past Tense**
I	am	was
You	are	were
She/he/it	is	was
We	are	were
You	are	were
They	are	were

Identify the five incorrect forms of the verb *be* in the draft. Write the correct form of the verb above the error. (2 points for each correction)

>   was
>   A long time ago, I were afraid of dogs. Every time I saw a dog I
>   ^
>
> would stand absolutely still. Nobody could make me move until the dog
> was   were
> were gone. I don't know why, but dogs was just frightening to me. My
> ^   ^
>   is
> aunt said she would help me get to know her dog, Maggie. Maggie are a
>   ^
>
> medium-sized dog. Every day for a month my aunt came to our house
>   was
> with Maggie. She were right. I began to trust Maggie and some other
>   ^
>
> dogs too.

Assessment Tip: Total **10** Points

Name _____

Writing a Clarification Composition

Sometimes when you read, you will encounter a quote or statement that expresses a belief but whose meaning is not entirely clear. You can write a **clarification composition** to clarify the statement.

Choose one of the following statements and write it on the clarification map:

► *The only thing we have to fear is fear itself.*
   (Franklin D. Roosevelt)
► *Fools rush in where angels fear to tread.*
   (Alexander Pope)
► *Anything is possible, but not everything is probable.*
   (Doug Grillo)

Then write what you think the statement means, and list reasons, details, and examples from *The Fear Place* that support your opinion. Answers will vary.

Statement (1 point)
Meaning (2)
Reasons, Details, and Examples (2)

On a separate sheet of paper, write a three- to five-paragraph composition restating the statement in your own words and clarifying its meaning. Use examples from *The Fear Place* that support your opinion. (5)

Name _____

Combining Sentences with Helping Verbs

Good writers avoid unnecessary repetition in their writing.
Sometimes you can improve your writing by combining
sentences that repeat the same helping verb into one sentence.

> He **had** reached the ledge. He **had** glanced down
> at the canyon.
>
> He **had** reached the ledge and glanced down at the
> canyon.

**Revise a postcard that Doug Grillo might have sent. Combine sentences that
repeat the same helping verb into a single sentence. Write the revised message
on the lines below. (2 points** for each combined sentence)

Dear Jim,

*We are finishing up our vacation in Colorado. We are coming home next week. I have
spotted a snowshoe rabbit. I have studied other wildlife for my merit badge. After a
fight, Gordie had hiked up a steep trail. My brother had pitched a tent on a high ridge.
I was very scared. I was determined to find my brother. I should have climbed with
someone else. I should have turned back before the narrow path curves sharply. Instead, I
faced my fear. With the help of Charlie the cougar, I reached my brother safely!*

Your friend,

Doug

We are finishing up our vacation in Colorado and coming home next week. I have

spotted a snowshoe rabbit and studied other wildlife for my merit badge. After a

fight, Gordie had hiked up a steep trail and pitched a tent on a high ridge. I was very

scared but determined to find my brother. I should have climbed with someone else

or turned back before the narrow path curves sharply. Instead, I faced my fear. With

the help of Charlie the cougar, I reached my brother safely!

Name _____

Space Is the Place

Write each word from the box on the correct line.

1. spacecraft

   satellite **(1 point)** _____

   space shuttle **(1)** _____

2. people

   specialist **(1)** _____

   astronaut **(1)** _____

3. descriptive words

   artificial **(1)** _____

   reusable **(1)** _____

4. words about movement

   launches **(1)** _____

   orbit **(1)** _____

5. a condition

   weightlessness **(1)** _____

Vocabulary

artificial

satellite

launches *(verb)*

orbit

reusable

mission

specialist

space shuttle

astronaut

weightlessness

Now choose three words from the box. Use them to write a short paragraph about the launch of a spacecraft.

(3) _____

_____

_____

_____

_____

_____

Main Idea Chart

Topic: Mae Jemison	
Page 211	On September 12, 1992, Mae Jemison became the first African American woman to fly into space.
Pages 212–213	When Mae Jemison was growing up, she was interested in space travel, science, and math. **(2 points)**
Pages 213–214	Mae Jemison became a doctor and joined the Peace Corps. **(2)**
Pages 215–216	Mae Jemison returned to her medical practice, took engineering courses, and was accepted by NASA. **(2)**
Page 217	At the end of her training, Mae Jemison became a mission specialist astronaut. **(2)**
Page 218	Mae Jemison became an astronaut herself aboard the space shuttle *Endeavour*. **(2)**
Pages 219–221	Mae Jamison conducted important experiments on space sickness and the effects of zero gravity. **(2)**
Pages 221–222	Mae Jamison resigned from the astronaut corps and formed a company whose goal is to improve the quality of life through science and technology. **(2)**

Assessment Tip: Total **14** Points

Is It True?

The sentences below tell about Mae Jemison. Write T if the sentence is true, or F if the sentence is false. If a sentence is false, tell why it is false.

1. Mae Jemison developed an interest in science at an early age.
   T **(2)**
   _____

   _____

2. Her parents and teachers all encouraged her to become a scientist.
   F One teacher told her she should try to become a nurse

   instead. **(2)**

3. When she graduated from Stanford University, she applied for admission to the astronaut corps.
   F She enrolled in medical school. **(2)**

   _____

4. Mae never gave up her childhood dream of traveling in space.
   T **(2)**
   _____

   _____

5. At the end of her year of intensive training, Mae Jemison rode a rocket into space.
   F After her year of training she had to wait four years to fly

   into space. **(2)**

6. On September 12, 1992, Mae Jemison became the first African American woman to journey into space.
   T **(2)**
   _____

Name _____

Exploring the Topic

Read the following passage. Then complete the activity on page 149.

Space Shuttle Science

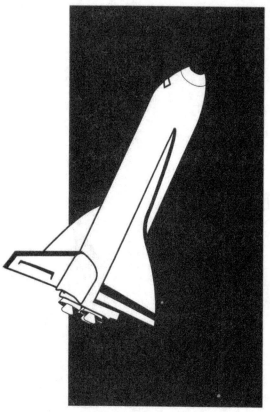

The space shuttle has many important uses. One use is for scientific research. In the weightless environment of space, scientists can carry out experiments they cannot do on Earth.

Inside the shuttle is a complete research laboratory called Spacelab. Spacelab is divided into two parts. One part is inside, where scientists can work. The other is outside and holds telescopes and other instruments that need to be exposed to space.

Most experiments take place in the inner section. Scientists on the space shuttle typically do experiments that make use of microgravity and weightlessness. They make new materials, such as crystals and silicon chips, and they also create medicines. Scientists even use themselves as test subjects, recording how weightlessness affects the human body.

Experiments in the outside section of Spacelab take advantage of being outside Earth's atmosphere. The atmosphere helps prevent radiation from reaching Earth, but it also makes radiation hard to study. Being outside the atmosphere also lets scientists use telescopes to get a clearer "view" of space.

Name _____

Exploring the Topic continued

Complete the chart below by filling in the topic and main ideas of the passage on page 148. Then write two details that support one of the main ideas.

Topic: Experiments on the Space Shuttle **(2 points)**

Main Ideas:	
first paragraph	1. Scientists use the space shuttle to do experiments they can't do on Earth. **(4)**
second paragraph	2. The research laboratory on the space shuttle is Spacelab. **(4)**
third paragraph	3. Most experiments inside Spacelab use microgravity and weightlessness. **(4)**
fourth paragraph	4. Experiments in the outside section take advantage of being outside Earth's atmosphere. **(4)**

Details:

1. The inside part of Spacelab is where scientists work. **(2)**

2. The outside part of Spacelab is for telescopes and other instruments that need to be exposed to space. **(2)**

Name _____

Suffix Shuttle

Choose words from the word boxes to write in the blanks in the paragraph below. Use the clue in parentheses to help you.

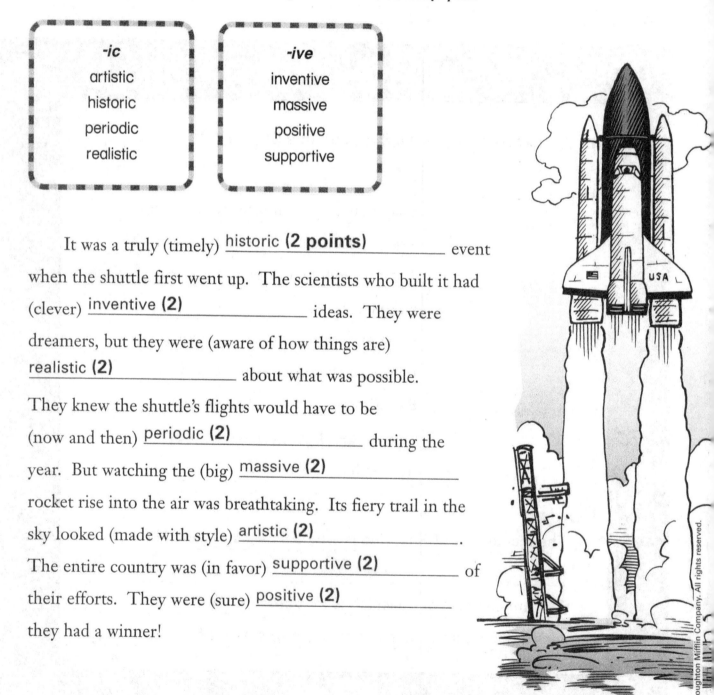

-ic	*-ive*
artistic	inventive
historic	massive
periodic	positive
realistic	supportive

It was a truly (timely) <u>historic **(2 points)**</u> event when the shuttle first went up. The scientists who built it had (clever) <u>inventive **(2)**</u> ideas. They were dreamers, but they were (aware of how things are) <u>realistic **(2)**</u> about what was possible. They knew the shuttle's flights would have to be (now and then) <u>periodic **(2)**</u> during the year. But watching the (big) <u>massive **(2)**</u> rocket rise into the air was breathtaking. Its fiery trail in the sky looked (made with style) <u>artistic **(2)**</u>. The entire country was (in favor) <u>supportive **(2)**</u> of their efforts. They were (sure) <u>positive **(2)**</u> they had a winner!

Assessment Tip: Total **16** Points

Name _____

The /ûr/ and /îr/ Sounds

When you hear the /ûr/ sound, think of the patterns *er, ir, ur, ear,*
and *or.* When you hear the /îr/ sounds, think of the patterns *eer*
and *ear.*

/ûr/ g**er**m, st**ir**, ret**ur**n, **ear**ly, w**or**th

/îr/ st**eer**, sm**ear**

▶ The /îr/ sound in *pier* differs from the usual spelling patterns.
In this word it is spelled *ier.*

Write each Spelling Word under its vowel + *r* sound.
Order of answers for each category may vary.

/ûr/ Sound

germ **(1 point)**	burnt **(1)**
return **(1)**	term **(1)**
stir **(1)**	pearl **(1)**
squirm **(1)**	squirt **(1)**
nerve **(1)**	perch **(1)**
early **(1)**	hurl **(1)**
worth **(1)**	worse **(1)**
thirst **(1)**	

/îr/ Sound

smear **(1)**	rear **(1)**
peer **(1)**	steer **(1)**
pier **(1)**	

Spelling Words

1. smear
2. germ
3. return
4. peer
5. stir
6. squirm
7. nerve
8. early
9. worth
10. pier*
11. thirst
12. burnt
13. rear
14. term
15. steer
16. pearl
17. squirt
18. perch
19. hurl
20. worse

Theme 2: **Give It All You've Got**   151
Assessment Tip: Total **20** Points

Name _____

Spelling Spree

Hint and Hunt Write the Spelling Word that answers each question.

1. What does a toy water pistol do?
2. What do you quench with a tall drink?
3. What is one thing you do with a spoon?
4. Where do you go to board a ship?
5. What might a diver find in an oyster?

1. squirt **(1 point)**
2. thirst **(1)**
3. stir **(1)**

4. pier **(1)**
5. pearl **(1)**

Word Maze Begin at the arrow and follow the Word Maze to find ten Spelling Words. Write the words in order below.

6. steer **(1)**
7. nerve **(1)**
8. burnt **(1)**

9. hurl **(1)**
10. rear **(1)**
11. germ **(1)**

12. smear **(1)**
13. term **(1)**
14. worse **(1)**
15. perch **(1)**

Spelling Words

1. smear
2. germ
3. return
4. peer
5. stir
6. squirm
7. nerve
8. early
9. worth
10. pier*
11. thirst
12. burnt
13. rear
14. term
15. steer
16. pearl
17. squirt
18. perch
19. hurl
20. worse

Assessment Tip: Total **15** Points

Name _____

Proofreading and Writing

Proofreading Circle the five misspelled Spelling Words in this part of a script for a class skit. Then write each word correctly.

Astronaut: Mission Control, when can we begin our (retern) to Earth?

Mission Control: Probably (erly) tomorrow morning. How's it going up there? How much fuel have you burnt?

Astronaut: Not much—we've still got a few days' (werth). We're all starting to (squerm) a bit up here, though. We're ready to go home. Actually, if I (per) closely through the glass here, I think I can see my house.

Mission Control: That's very funny.

---

1. return **(1 point)**
2. early **(1)**
3. worth **(1)**
4. squirm **(1)**
5. peer **(1)**

Write a Newspaper Article You have been asked to write a brief article about Mae Jemison's space shuttle mission for the school newspaper. Did any one of the experiments particularly interest you? Will you include any details about Jemison's personal life?

On a separate piece of paper, write your article about Mae Jemison's mission. Use Spelling Words from the list. Responses will vary. **(5)**

Stress on Syllables

Read each dictionary entry. Sound out the entry word three ways, placing stress on a different syllable each time. Circle the choice with the correct stress. (1 point each)

1. ad/ven/ture (ăd věn chər) *n.* A bold, dangerous, or risky undertaking.
   AD/ven/ture   (ad/VEN/ture)   ad/ven/TURE

2. en/gi/neer/ing (ĕn jə nîr ing) *n.* The practical use of scientific knowledge.
   EN/gi/neer/ing   en/GI/neer/ing   (en/gi/NEER/ing)

3. en/vi/ron/ment (ĕn vī rən mənt) *n.* Surroundings and conditions that affect the growth of living things.
   (en/VI/ron/ment)   en/vi/RON/ment   en/vi/ron/MENT

4. in/flu/ence (ĭn flōo əns) *n.* The power to have an effect without using direct force.
   (IN/flu/ence)   in/FLU/ence   in/flu/ENCE

5. or/gan/i/za/tion (ôr gən ĭ zā shən) *n.* A group of people united for some purpose or work.
   OR/gan/i/za/tion   or/GAN/i/za/tion   (or/gan/i/ZA/tion)

6. par/tic/i/pate (pär tĭs ə pāt) *v.* To join with others in doing something; take part.
   (par/TIC/i/pate)   par/tic/I/pate   par/tic/i/PATE

7. tel/e/vi/sion (tĕl ə vĭ zhən) *n.* The transmission and reception of visual images and sounds as electrical waves through the air or through wires.
   (TEL/e/vi/sion)   tel/e/VI/sion   tel/e/vi/SION

8. vol/un/teer (vŏl ən tîr) *n.* A person who performs a service of his or her own free will.
   VOL/un/teer   vol/UN/teer   (vol/un/TEER)

Assessment Tip: Total **8 Points**

Name _____

Astronauts Travel into Space

Verb Tenses Verbs have forms, or tenses, that tell when the action occurs.

► A **present-tense** verb shows action that happens now, or that happens regularly over time.

► A **past-tense** verb shows that something already occurred.

► To form the **present tense,** add *-s* or *-es* to most verbs if the subject is singular. Do not add *-s* or *-es* if the subject is plural or *I* or *you*.

► To form the **past tense** of most verbs, add *-ed*.

On the line, write the tense of the verb in the first sentence of each pair. Then fill in the blank of the second sentence with the same verb, but change its tense.

Example: Astronauts conducted experiments in space. ___past___

Astronauts ___conduct___ experiments in space.

1. My mother studies engineering at the university. ___present **(1 point)**___

   My mother ___studied **(1)**___ engineering at the university.

2. You learned about space travel in school. ___past **(1)**___

   You ___learn **(1)**___ about space travel in school.

3. I worked hard on my science project. ___past **(1)**___

   I ___work **(1)**___ hard on my science project.

4. Kate's father designs bridges. ___present **(1)**___

   Kate's father ___designed **(1)**___ bridges.

5. She followed her dreams. ___past **(1)**___

   She ___follows **(1)**___ her dreams.

Name _____

Astronauts Will Travel into Space

More about Verbs A **future-tense** verb shows that something is going to happen. Form the **future tense** by using the helping verb *will* or *shall* with the main verb.

> **Present Tense:** I **see** many films about space.
>
> **Future Tense:** I **will see** many films about space.
>
> **Present Tense:** He **reads** about Jupiter.
>
> **Future Tense:** He **shall read** about Jupiter.

Rewrite each sentence. Change each verb from the present or past tense to the future tense.

> **Example:** You go to Cape Canaveral.
>
> *You will go to Cape Canaveral.*

1. Astronauts fly the space shuttle.
   Astronauts will fly the space shuttle. **(2 points)**

2. The space probe landed on Mars.
   The space probe will land on Mars. **(2)**

3. You studied physics in college.
   You will study physics in college. **(2)**

4. Meteors shoot across the sky.
   Meteors will shoot across the sky. **(2)**

5. We think about the future.
   We will think about the future. **(2)**

Assessment Tip: Total **10** Points

Name _____

I Joined

Using the Right Tense A good writer uses the correct tense to talk about a particular time. Look at the two examples below. The second sentence in each pair makes more sense than the first sentence.

Incorrect: I will clean my room yesterday.
Correct: I cleaned my room yesterday.
Incorrect: Next Thursday Jeremy listens to me on the radio.
Correct: Next Thursday Jeremy will listen to me on the radio.

George has written a paragraph about his dream of joining the Peace Corps, like Mae Jemison and his teacher. Revise the paragraph to correct problems with verb tenses.

(**2 points** each)

will go
Example: Next week, we went to South America.
　　　　　　　　　　　　　　　^

　　　　　　　　　will join
　　Someday, I joined the Peace Corps. Last month, my teacher Mr.
　　talked　　　^
Stinson talks about his experience as a member of the Peace Corps in
　　　showed
Ghana. He shows us photographs of the region too. He made many
　　　　^

new friends while he was there. In the Peace Corps, my teacher
　worked　　　　　　　　　　　　　　　　*ask*
will work to help build a school. Every day now I asked him to tell us
　　^　　　　　　　　　　　　　　　　　　　　^

more about it.

Writing a Business Letter

When Mae Jemison applied to the National Aeronautics and Space
Administration to become an astronaut, she wrote a business letter. You
write a **business letter** to apply for a job, to request or persuade
someone to do something, to order a product from ads or catalogs, to ask
for information, to complain about a product or service, or to express an
opinion to a newspaper, or to a radio or TV station.

**On a separate sheet of paper, plan and organize a business letter.
Either write a letter of recommendation to NASA telling why Mae
Jemison would make an excellent astronaut, or write to a company
asking for information. Follow these steps:**

1. Write a **heading** (your own address and the date) in the upper right
   corner.
2. Write the **inside address** (the address of the person or business you
   are writing to) at the left margin.
3. Write a **greeting** (*Dear Sir or Madam:* or *Dear [business name]:)* at the
   left margin below the inside address.
4. Write the **body** of your letter below the greeting. Be brief and direct,
   but present all of the necessary details clearly. If you state an opinion,
   support it with details. If you order a product, identify the item, size,
   color, price, and quantity you want. Make sure to use a formal and
   polite tone.
5. Write a formal **closing** such as *Sincerely, Cordially,* or *Yours truly* in
   the lower right corner.
6. Sign your full name under the closing. Then print or type your name
   below your **signature**.

**When you finish planning your business letter, copy it onto a clean
sheet of paper. Then share it with a classmate or send it to the
company you wrote to.** (**2 points** for each part of the letter)

Name _____

Using the Right Tone

Tone is the attitude that a writer has toward a subject and is conveyed in the choice of words and details. Here are some tips to follow when you write a business letter:

▶ Use polite language and a formal tone.

▶ Use correct grammar and complete sentences.

▶ Avoid the use of slang.

▶ Do not include personal information.

Fill in the chart with examples of language and details that do *not* strike the proper tone.

> 144 Primrose Street
> Evanston, IL 60201
> October 23, 2001
>
> Dr. Mae Jemison
> P.O. Box 591455
> Houston, TX 77259-1455
> Dear Mae,
>
>   I am in the fifth grade at Primrose Elementary School. My class will be studying about space and space travel. I got a 91 on my last quiz. We hope you might be able to come talk to our class about your experiences as an astronaut.
>
>   It would be the bomb to meet an astronaut in person. My uncle is a pilot. We look forward to hearing from you. Do not give us some lame excuse about why you cannot speak here.
>
>   Love,
>   *Karen Aldrin*

Slang: the bomb **(2 points)**

Impolite Language: Do not give us some lame excuse about why you cannot speak here. **(2)**

Informal Tone: Dear Mae, Love **(2)**

Personal Information: I got a 91 on my last quiz; My uncle is a pilot. **(2)**

160

Name _____

Iditarod History

Use the words in the box to complete the article about the Iditarod Trail Race.

> ···· **Vocabulary** ····
>
> obstacles   spectators   pace   musher   checkpoint   cargo

The Iditarod Trail Sled Dog Race celebrates one of the most famous events in Alaska's history. In 1925, a serious illness struck the city of Nome. The closest supply of medicine was far across the state in Anchorage. Twenty men drove their dog teams up the Iditarod Trail in a long relay. Each musher **(2 points)** drove his team at a fast pace **(2)** to bring the medicine to Nome. The precious cargo **(2)** of medicine arrived in Nome only a week after it left Anchorage.

In the late 1960s, several Alaskans wanted to honor their state's 100th anniversary. They proposed a dog sled race along the Iditarod Trail. The U.S. Army helped clear the old trail of obstacles **(2)**, and in 1973, the first modern Iditarod race was held.

Today, volunteers inspect and monitor the teams at over twenty checkpoints **(2)** along the trail. Thousands of spectators **(2)** line the racecourse to watch the competition.

Name _____

What Will Happen?

Fill in this Predicting Outcomes chart as you read the Paired Selections. Accept reasonable answers. Sample answers are given.

	Iditarod Dream	*Me, Mop, and the Moondance Kid*
Details about the main character	1. He loves racing. **(1 point)** 2. He knows how to handle a sled. **(1)** 3. He keeps his head when he gets into trouble. **(1)**	1. He has trouble catching the ball. **(1)** 2. He has trouble hitting. **(1)** 3. He is scared of getting hit by the ball. **(1)**
Details about the character's team	1. They pull hard. **(1)** 2. Dusty takes care of them. **(1)**	1. Moondance pitches the ball fast. **(1)** 2. Sister Carmelita is trying to help them. **(1)**
What will happen after the selection ends?	Dusty will decide to race in the real Iditarod. **(1)**	T.J.'s team will start doing better, but T.J. will still have trouble playing baseball. **(1)**

Assessment Tip: Total **12** Points

Name _____

Discuss Photographs

Use the chart below to compare and contrast the photographs in this theme. Sample answers are provided. Accept reasonable responses.

Iditarod Dream

Photographs	What Is Shown	How the Photos Add to the Story
page 230C	Dusty and his team starting the race (1 point)	They show story events in sequence. They help readers see what Dusty goes through. (2 points)
page 230G	Dusty doing chores at Yentna Station (1)	
page 230I	Dusty and his parents after his victory (1)	

Michelle Kwan: Heart of a Champion

Photographs	What Is Shown	How the Photos Add to the Story
page 141	Michelle skating at the 1992 Nationals (1)	They show important events and influences in Michelle Kwan's life. They help readers understand what makes her a champion. (2)
page 142	Michelle practicing with her coach, Frank Carroll (1)	
page 145	Champion skaters Dorothy Hamill, Brian Boitano, and Peggy Fleming (1)	

Mae Jemison: Space Scientist

Photographs	What Is Shown	How the Photos Add to the Story
page 212	Mae and her team on their 1987 space shuttle mission (1)	They show the different jobs Mae Jemison has held. They show readers that she has done interesting work throughout her life. (2)
page 214	Mae working as a doctor before she became an astronaut (1)	
page 222	Mae congratulating a young contest winner (1)	

Name _____

Fly Ball Words

Use the words from the box to complete the sentences below.

Vocabulary

inning	play-offs	backstop
foul	respectable	control

- When each team makes three outs, the <u>inning **(2 points)**</u> is over.
- The best pitchers have great <u>control **(2)**</u>. They can put the ball wherever they want.
- The catcher fields most <u>foul **(2)**</u> pop-ups between home plate and the <u>backstop **(2)**</u>.
- Only teams with a <u>respectable **(2)**</u> number of wins make the league <u>play-offs **(2)**</u> at the end of the season.

Now use four of the vocabulary words in sentences of your own.

<u>Answers will vary, but should include four vocabulary words. **(1 point**</u>
<u>for each word used correctly**)**</u>

_____

_____

164   Theme 2: **Give It All You've Got**
Assessment Tip: Total **16** Points

Name _____

Test Practice

Use the three steps you've learned to complete these sentences about *Me, Mop, and the Moondance Kid*. Fill in the circle for the best answer in the answer row at the bottom of the page.

1. *Me, Mop, and the Moondance Kid* is told from the point of view of

    _____.

    A T.J.   **C** Moondance

    B Mop   **D** Dad

2. Dad is discouraged with the Elks because they _____.

    F do not take his advice   **H** do not have a good coach

    G do not show his sons respect   **J** are not playing well

3. Moondance's pitching problem is that _____.

    A he gets nervous when others are watching

    B he is afraid of hitting someone with the ball

    C he does not throw the ball fast enough

    D he does not listen to advice from others

4. **Connecting/Comparing** Think about *Me, Mop, and the Moondance Kid* and *Iditarod Dream*. T.J. and Dusty are alike in that both boys

    _____.

    F are overly confident about their abilities

    G blame their failures on others

    H make a mistake during a competition

    J feel they have disappointed their parents

ANSWER ROWS   1 Ⓐ Ⓑ Ⓒ Ⓓ **(5 points)**   3 Ⓐ Ⓑ Ⓒ Ⓓ **(5)**
                     2 Ⓕ Ⓖ Ⓗ Ⓙ **(5)**   4 Ⓕ Ⓖ Ⓗ Ⓙ **(5)**

Continue on page 166.

Name _____

Test Practice continued

5. Dad asks Sister Carmelita to help Moondance because she

   _____.

   A used to be a good pitcher   **C** is a Little League coach

   B played professional baseball **D** likes to help others

6. Moondance probably feels that he _____.

   F can be a good pitcher without Titi's help

   G should play basketball instead

   H can become a professional baseball player

   J will never be good enough to please Dad

7. The author wrote *Me, Mop, and the Moondance Kid* in order to

   _____.

   A tell a story about two sons and their father

   B persuade young people to play baseball

   C tell the story of a professional baseball player

   D describe how to pitch a baseball

8. **Connecting/Comparing** Both Moondance and Michelle Kwan

   understand that _____.

   F coaches don't always give the best advice

   G parents can expect too much from children

   H improving your performance can be challenging

   J performing for an audience is fun

ANSWER ROWS 5 Ⓐ Ⓑ Ⓒ Ⓓ **(5 points)** 7 Ⓐ Ⓑ Ⓒ Ⓓ **(5)**

6 Ⓕ Ⓖ Ⓗ Ⓙ **(5)** 8 Ⓕ Ⓖ Ⓗ Ⓙ **(5)**

Assessment Tip: Total **40** Points

Name _____

Fact or Opinion?

Read each statement below. Write *F* if the statement is a fact and *O* if the statement is an opinion.

1. The Junior Iditarod is two days long. F **(1 point)**

2. It is the hardest sled dog race in all of Alaska. O **(1)**

3. The race winds along a trail in the forest. F **(1)**

4. Sled dogs are small but very strong. F **(1)**

5. I believe snowmobiles should stay off the race course. O **(1)**

6. A musher's worst nightmare is running into a moose. O **(1)**

7. Sled drivers sometimes run alongside their sleds. F **(1)**

8. When racers reach the halfway point, they must stay with their dogs.
F **(1)**

9. The most difficult part of the race is near the finish line. O **(1)**

10. You must win the race to have fun. O **(1)**

Name _____

What's It All About?

Read the passage below. Then complete the chart by filling in the topic and main ideas. Also add two details from the passage that support each main idea.

The Iditarod Trail Sled Dog Race takes place each winter in Alaska. It is run on a 1,150-mile trail from Anchorage to Nome. Mushers and dog teams cover the distance in about 10 to 17 days. They cross frozen rivers and lakes. They make their way through dense forests and past jagged mountains. The temperature is often well below zero degrees Fahrenheit.

The first Iditarod Trail Race took place in 1973. All twenty-two mushers were men. Almost all were from Alaska. The very next year women joined the race, and Mary Shields became the first woman to finish, placing 23rd. In 1985, Libby Riddles became the first woman to win the Iditarod. Since its beginnings, the race has welcomed mushers from more than 20 states and 13 nations, including Japan, Australia, and Czechoslovakia. In 2003, the winner was Robert Sørlie, a firefighter from Norway, who became the second non-Alaskan to win the race. Details and wording of responses may vary.

Topic: Iditarod Sled Dog Race **(2 points)**
Main Idea: The Iditarod Trail Sled Dog Race is a difficult challenge. **(2)**
Details: They cross frozen rivers. The temperature is below zero. **(2)**
Main Idea: The race has attracted men and women racers from many different places. **(2)**
Details:
Mushers came from 20 states. In 2003, a firefighter from
Norway won. **(2)**

Assessment Tip: Total **10** Points

Name _____

Find the Suffix

Read the sentences. Underline the word in each sentence with the suffix -*ous* or the suffix -*ward*. Then write the meaning of the word.
Wording of definitions will vary.

1. My uncle told me a <u>humorous</u> story from his youth.
   <u>full of humor **(1 point)**</u>

2. The story began on a train moving <u>westward</u> from Denver.
   <u>to the west **(1)**</u>

3. The train soon entered <u>mountainous</u> country.
   <u>full of mountains **(1)**</u>

4. The train made a <u>continuous</u> *clickity-clack* as it passed over the rails.
   <u>characterized by continuing **(1)**</u>

5. Suddenly the train came to a stop and began moving <u>backward</u>.
   <u>in reverse **(1)**</u>

6. My uncle glanced <u>anxiously</u> at the other passengers.
   <u>characterized by anxiety **(1)**</u>

7. A little later the train started moving <u>forward</u> again.
   <u>ahead **(1)**</u>

8. The conductor entered the car with a <u>tremendous</u> smile on his face.
   <u>very large **(1)**</u>

9. The engineer had seen a <u>poisonous</u> snake on the tracks and was
   backing away from it. <u>full of poison **(1)**</u>

10. "That was simply <u>ridiculous</u>," my uncle said. "He could have scared
    it with the whistle." <u>full of ridicule **(1)**</u>

Name _____

Write the Right Word!

Read the homophone pairs and the sentence next to them. Use context to help you figure out which word to write in each blank.

1. ant/aunt   My _aunt **1 point)**_____ found an
   _ant **(1)**_____ in her kitchen.

2. read/red   We _read **(1)**_____ about
   _red **(1)**_____ and white blood cells for science class.

3. close/clothes   _Close **(1)**_____ the dryer before all the
   _clothes **(1)**_____ tumble out!

4. hall/haul   You'll have to _haul **(1)**_____ your suitcase to your
   room down the _hall **(1)**_____.

5. soar/sore   Even with a _sore **(1)**_____ wing, the hawk could
   _soar **(1)**_____ high overhead.

6. tide/tied   The girls _tied **(1)**_____ up the boat so it wouldn't
   drift out on the _tide **(1)**_____.

7. blew/blue   Jacqueline _blew **(1)**_____ the
   _blue **(1)**_____ candle out.

8. knew/new   Wes _knew **(1)**_____ the school had a
   _new **(1)**_____ gymnasium.

9. their/there   How many students left _their **(1)**_____ jackets
   _there **(1)**_____?

10. wait/weight   Dana's little brother couldn't _wait **(1)**_____
    until his _weight **(1)**_____ reached 40 pounds.

Assessment Tip: Total **20** Points

Name _____

Spelling Review

Write Spelling Words from the list on this page to answer the questions.

Order of answers in each category may vary.

1–8. Which eight words have the /ou/, /ô/, or /oi/ sounds?

1. halt **(1 point)**

2. thousand **(1)**

3. brother-in-law **(1)**

4. noisy **(1)**

5. launch **(1)**

6. hawk **(1)**

7. royal **(1)**

8. coward **(1)**

9–26. Which eighteen words have the /ôr/, /âr/, /är/, /ûr/, or /îr/ sounds?

9. gorge **(1)**

10. wheelchair **(1)**

11. soar **(1)**

12. tore **(1)**

13. snare **(1)**

14. flair **(1)**

15. carve **(1)**

16. barge **(1)**

17. steer **(1)**

18. first aid **(1)**

19. smear **(1)**

20. hurl **(1)**

21. perch **(1)**

22. early **(1)**

23. worth **(1)**

24. pearl **(1)**

25. stir **(1)**

26. return **(1)**

27–30. Which four compound words have one of these words in them?

    end   wild   test   date

27. weekend **(1)**

28. wildlife **(1)**

29. test tube **(1)**

30. up-to-date **(1)**

Spelling Words

1. halt
2. weekend
3. steer
4. gorge
5. first aid
6. smear
7. thousand
8. wildlife
9. hurl
10. brother-in-law
11. perch
12. test tube
13. wheelchair
14. early
15. noisy
16. launch
17. hawk
18. royal
19. worth
20. soar
21. pearl
22. up-to-date
23. tore
24. stir
25. snare
26. flair
27. carve
28. barge
29. coward
30. return

Assessment Tip: Total **30** Points

Name _____

Spelling Spree

Rhyme Time Write a Spelling Word that rhymes with the underlined word and makes sense in the sentence.

1. Marge, do you see that large barge **(1 point)** _____ ?

2. Howard, how did you spell the word coward **(1)** _____ ?

3. If the plane will soar **(1)** _____, we will roar.

4. Let us forge ahead through the narrow gorge **(1)** _____.

5. I wore my new shirt until it tore **(1)** _____.

6. Please hurl **(1)** _____ the ball to the girl with the curl.

7. Nate, please rate our new up-to-date **(1)** _____ gate.

The Third Word Write the Spelling Word that belongs in each group.

8. to come back, to revisit, to return **(1)** _____

9. diamond, ruby, pearl **(1)** _____

10. sister-in-law, father-in-law, brother-in-law **(1)** _____

11. to balance, to wobble, to perch **(1)** _____

12. ten, hundred, thousand **(1)** _____

13. days off, holiday, weekend **(1)** _____

14. to start, to begin, to launch **(1)** _____

15. animals, nature, wildlife **(1)** _____

Spelling Words

1. weekend
2. coward
3. soar
4. up-to-date
5. brother-in-law
6. gorge
7. tore
8. thousand
9. wildlife
10. barge
11. launch
12. return
13. perch
14. pearl
15. hurl

Assessment Tip: Total **15** Points

Name _____

Proofreading and Writing

Proofreading Circle the six misspelled Spelling Words in this diary entry. Then write each word correctly.

April 18—This weekend I woke up (erly) to go to the race. At the track, I passed the (first ade) station and steered my (weelchair) into place at the starting line. The crowd was (noysy.) I didn't win, but I felt like a (royel) princess when I came to a (hault) at the finish line.

1. early **(1 point)**
2. first aid **(1)**
3. wheelchair **(1)**
4. noisy **(1)**
5. royal **(1)**
6. halt **(1)**

Spelling Words

1. halt
2. noisy
3. early
4. hawk
5. test tube
6. snare
7. wheelchair
8. flair
9. steer
10. carve
11. stir
12. worth
13. smear
14. royal
15. first aid

Revise a Letter Write Spelling Words to complete the letter.

You should have seen me steer **(1)** through the pack during the race! I flew like a hawk **(1)** . Then I felt like I was caught in a snare **(1)** when I hit some loose gravel. I recovered quickly. Racing is hard, but it is worth **(1)** the effort. I have a real flair **(1)** for it, I think.

School was fun today. For art class, I started to carve **(1)** a horse out of soap. Then in science I had to stir **(1)** a solution and put it in a test tube **(1)** . Last, we had to smear **(1)** pond water on a slide and look at it under a microscope.

✏️ **Write an Article** On a separate sheet of paper, write a short newspaper article about a race or sport you enjoy. Use the **Spelling Review Words.** Responses will vary. **(5)**

Name _____

Working with Common, Proper, and Possessive Nouns

Copy the nouns from the following sentences into the appropriate columns below. When you rewrite a proper noun, be sure to capitalize correctly.

1. Dusty has many good dogs.
2. This young musher heads for the Iditarod Trail.
3. The team must pull the sled safely back to Wasilla.
4. The snow is usually deep in January and February.

Common Nouns	Proper Nouns
dogs **(1 point)**	Dusty **(1)**
musher **(1)**	Iditarod Trail **(1)**
team **(1)**	Wasilla **(1)**
sled **(1)**	January **(1)**
snow **(1)**	February **(1)**

Complete each sentence by writing the possessive form of the noun shown in parentheses. Circle each plural possessive noun you write.

5. The _musher's_ **(1)** feet are cold. (musher)
6. The _dogs'_ **(1)** coats are thick. (dogs)
7. The _handlers'_ **(1)** faces are red. (handlers)
8. The _sled's_ **(1)** runners are icy. (sled)
9. The _winner's_ **(1)** smile shows his happiness. (winner)

Assessment Tip: Total **15** Points

Name _____

Identifying Action Verbs and Direct Objects

Underline each action verb. Circle each direct object. Not every sentence has a direct object.

1. The pitcher <u>throws</u> the (ball.) **(1 point)**
2. The batter <u>swings</u> hard. **(1)**
3. She <u>hits</u> a long (fly.) **(1)**
4. The right fielder <u>raises</u> his (glove.) **(1)**
5. The ball <u>flies</u> over the glove. **(1)**
6. The ball <u>bounces</u> to the fence. **(1)**
7. The right fielder <u>grabs</u> the (ball.) **(1)**
8. He <u>fires</u> a (bullet) to the third baseman. **(1)**
9. The third baseman <u>tags</u> the (runner.) **(1)**
10. The runner <u>touched</u> the (base) before the tag. **(1)**

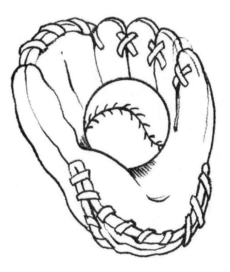

Theme 2: **Give It All You've Got** 175
Assessment Tip: Total **10** Points

Copyright © Houghton Mifflin Company. All rights reserved.

Name _____

Poetry Pen Pals

Use words from the box to complete the letter below.

January 21, 2002

Dear Amy,

Hi! How are you? I am starting to enjoy my new home in Pennsylvania, but I still miss Hillside Elementary very much. I also miss the warm weather! I have been writing a lot since we moved. I am sending you a <u>poem</u> **(1 point)** to read that I wrote a few months ago. I tried to make the last word in each line <u>rhyme</u> **(1)** , but sometimes the words were too unusual. The poem is about taking a walk in the winter, and I tried to create the <u>rhythm</u> **(1)** and sound of feet walking in crunchy snow. My favorite <u>image</u> **(1)** is of the snow swirling around the streetlights. I would love to hear what you think about it. I found out that writing poetry takes a lot of creativity and <u>imagination</u> **(1)** ! Please let me know if you like it. I miss you!

Your friend,

Wendy

Write a short reply from Amy to Wendy, using each of the vocabulary words at least once. (1 point per genre vocabulary word**)**

Vocabulary

poem
rhythm
rhyme
imagination
image

_____

_____

_____

_____

_____

_____

Name _____

Elements of Poetry

Look for these elements in the poems Sample answers are given.

Places and Seasons: List words that show sensory details.

Poem _"Lemon Tree"_ **(1 point)**	Poem knoxville, tennessee **(1)**
feel the bark/under your knees and feet; smell the white flowers **(1)**	eat fresh corn; lots of barbecue and buttermilk and home-made ice cream; go barefooted and be warm all the time **(1)**

Animals: List rhyme patterns and repetition.

Poem _"Whirligig Beetles"_ **(1)**	Poem _"It's All the Same to the Clam"_ **(1)**
rhymes using the *-ing* sound, repeats many words **(1)**	repeats the title line, rhyme pattern ABABCCCB **(1)**

People: List words that describe the mood.

Poem _"Campfire"_ **(1)**	Poem _"Reggie"_ **(1)**
respectful, suspenseful, humorous **(1)**	wistful, sad **(1)**

Assessment Tip: Total **12** Points

Name _____

Two Poems

Choose two poems: one that rhymes and follows a pattern, and one that doesn't, called free verse. On the chart below, compare the two poems by answering the questions. Sample answers shown.

	Rhyming Poem Travel _____ Title	**Free Verse Poem** Lemon Tree _____ Title
What is the poem about?	It is about the poet's love of train travel. **(3 points)**	It is about climbing a tree and using all your senses. **(3)**
What word or sound patterns are in the poem?	In each stanza, lines 1 and 3 rhyme and lines 2 and 4 rhyme. **(3)**	The poet repeats verbs and uses short phrases. **(3)**
What word pictures does the poem create?	It creates a word picture of a train at night, in the distance, puffing smoke and cinders. **(3)**	It creates a picture of a lemon tree with white blossoms and rough bark and branches. **(3)**

Assessment Tip: Total **18** Points

Name _____

Poetry Award

You are the poetry editor for a magazine. Choose one poem from *Focus on Poetry* **as the Poem of the Year. Tell what makes it a good poem and why people will want to read it.**

Answers will vary.

Poem of the Year

_____

I think this poem is the best because

_____

_____

_____

_____

_____

_____

_____

_____

_____

_____

_____

_____

_____

_____

_____

(Total **10 Points** for using details from the poem)

Assessment Tip: Total **10 Points**

Analyzing a Poem

Choose another poem to study closely. Make notes about sensory words, rhyme, repetition, and mood on the chart. Then write a paragraph that describes how the poem uses each of these elements. Use examples to support your ideas.

Poem: _Answers will vary._ _____

Sensory Words	**(2 points)**
Rhyme	**(2)**
Repetition	**(2)**
Mood	**(2)**

_____

_____

_____

_____

_____

_____ **(4)**

Name _____

Poetic Dreams

Read this diary entry. In the underlined words, circle the suffixes -ward, -ous, -ive, and ic. (1 point each)

Dear Diary,

We wrote poems in class today. The teacher told us to think of a joy**ous** or memorable experience from our lives. She reminded us to use act**ive**, lively language with vivid images. I was leaning to**ward** writing about the wondr**ous** landscape I saw during my trip to the mountains. The teacher called out instruct**ive** hints as we wrote, but I was still having trouble getting started. I decided to read the work of some histor**ic** poets for inspiration. I read a few poems by Robert Frost and Emily Dickinson, and then I was excited to start my own. I wrote about the long, continu**ous** path we hiked in the mountains. I described the marvel**ous** views and the sense of peace I felt as we hiked down**ward**. When I finished the poem, I was very happy with it. Maybe someday I will be a fam**ous** poet!

Now, write each underlined word from the diary entry beside its correct definition.

1. famous **(1)** _____ : well known

2. toward **(1)** _____ : in the direction of

3. instructive **(1)** _____ : relating to knowledge or skill

4. marvelous **(1)** _____ : causing wonder or astonishment

5. active **(1)** _____ : full of energy

6. continuous **(1)** _____ : going on without stopping

7. downward **(1)** _____ : from a higher to a lower place

8. wondrous **(1)** _____ : marvelous; remarkable

9. joyous **(1)** _____ : full of delight and pleasure

10. historic **(1)** _____ : important or famous in history

Assessment Tip: Total **20** Points

Name _____

Homophones

Remember that homophones are words that sound alike but have different spellings and meanings.

/pān/ **pain** "physical suffering caused by injury"

/pān/ **pane** "a sheet of glass"

Write each pair of Spelling Words under the heading that names their vowel sound.

Order of answers for each category may vary.

/ā/ Sound

pray **(1 point)**

prey **(1)**

pain **(1)**

pane **(1)**

/ē/ Sound

seam **(1)**

seem **(1)**

piece **(1)**

peace **(1)**

peel **(1)**

peal **(1)**

/ō/ Sound

sole **(1)**

soul **(1)**

role **(1)**

roll **(1)**

shone **(1)**

shown **(1)**

pole **(1)**

poll **(1)**

/ôr/ Sounds

cord **(1)**

chord **(1)**

Spelling Words

1. cord
2. chord
3. pray
4. prey
5. seam
6. seem
7. sole
8. soul
9. piece
10. peace
11. role
12. roll
13. peel
14. peal
15. shone
16. shown
17. pain
18. pane
19. pole
20. poll

Assessment Tip: Total **20** Points

Name _____

Spelling Spree

Book Titles Write the Spelling Word that correctly completes each book title. Remember to use capital letters.

1. <u>Roll **(1 point)**</u> Over! 50 Dog Tricks by K. Nyne

2. How Lions Hunt for <u>Prey **(1)**</u> by Tawny Katz

3. The Torn <u>Seam **(1)**</u>: A Guide for Tailors by So Ng

4. Love, <u>Peace **(1)**</u>, and Happiness by Flow R. Child

5. My Starring <u>Role **(1)**</u> in Movies by I. M. Cool

6. How to Fix the <u>Sole **(1)**</u> of a Shoe by Cobb Lurr

7. Using Every Potato <u>Peel **(1)**</u>: Learning to Compost by Rich Soyl

8. The Sun <u>Shone **(1)**</u> Down by Clair Skye

9. The Broken <u>Pane **(1)**</u> of Glass by Ike N. Ficksitt

10. Play That <u>Chord **(1)**</u>: A Beginner's Guide to the Guitar by Ivana Strumm

Hidden Words Write the Spelling Word that is hidden in each row of letters. Don't let the other words fool you!

11. leapollocal   <u>poll **(1)**</u>
12. francorder   <u>cord **(1)**</u>
13. classoulilby   <u>soul **(1)**</u>
14. blimprayellow   <u>pray **(1)**</u>
15. blesseempire   <u>seem **(1)**</u>

16. trapoless   <u>pole **(1)**</u>
17. cashownersh   <u>shown **(1)**</u>
18. propaincons   <u>pain **(1)**</u>
19. capiecertay   <u>piece **(1)**</u>
20. appealisie   <u>peal **(1)**</u>

Spelling Words

1. cord
2. chord
3. pray
4. prey
5. seam
6. seem
7. sole
8. soul
9. piece
10. peace
11. role
12. roll
13. peel
14. peal
15. shone
16. shown
17. pain
18. pane
19. pole
20. poll

Assessment Tip: Total **20 Points**

Name _____

Proofreading and Writing

Proofreading **Circle the five misspelled Spelling Words in this poem. Then write each word correctly.**

Order of answers may vary.

Lighten Up

Through the (paine) of dirty glass,
Dark clouds glowered.
I felt listless, sad, grumpy.
Then, with the energy of a small child,
A (seme) of sunlight (shoon) through the clouds,
Bursting through the gloom.
That sole (peice) of light
Wakened my (sol,) calling,
"Lighten up!"

1. pane **(1 point)**
2. seam **(1)**
3. shone **(1)**
4. piece **(1)**
5. soul **(1)**

Spelling Words

1. cord
2. chord
3. pray
4. prey
5. seam
6. seem
7. sole
8. soul
9. piece
10. peace
11. role
12. roll
13. peel
14. peal
15. shone
16. shown
17. pain
18. pane
19. pole
20. poll

➤ **Write a Song** The words to many songs are often very poetic. The songwriter may express feelings or send a message to listeners. Think of a topic that you would like to write a song about, and think of a favorite tune.

On a separate sheet of paper, write new song lyrics to go with a familiar tune. Use Spelling Words from the list.

Responses will vary. **(5 points)**

Name _____

Borrowed Language

**Read each entry word, its origin, and its definition on the dictionary
page below. Then fill in the correct word in each sentence below.**

> **caveat** (Latin): a warning or explanation
>
> **cuisine** (French): a particular type of cooking
>
> **encore** (French): an additional performance
>
> **habitat** (Latin): the place or environment where a person or
> thing is most likely to live
>
> **memento** (Latin): something that serves as a reminder
>
> **modus operandi** (Latin): a way of operating or functioning
>
> **pronto** (Spanish): without delay; quickly
>
> **siesta** (Spanish): a nap

1. After thunderous applause from the audience, the singer reappeared
   on stage and agreed to do an __encore **(1 point)**__.

2. She keeps an old pink slipper as a __memento **(1)**__ of her
   dancing days.

3. Leo's unusual __modus operandi **(1)**__ makes no sense to his coworkers,
   who prefer not to do everything backward.

4. If we don't get moving __pronto **(1)**__, we won't get to the
   bake sale before the cookies are gone.

5. I have just one __caveat **(1)**__: if I can't have dessert, I won't
   eat my spinach.

6. I yawned and took a __siesta **(1)**__ during the opera star's
   performance.

7. My lizard, Eddie, prefers a dry, desert-like __habitat **(1)**__.

8. Eddie's favorite __cuisine **(1)**__ is Chinese takeout, although
   he enjoys French food too.

Assessment Tip: Total **8** Points

Name _____

A Family of Poets

Capitalizing Nouns That Replace Names Use a capital letter with a
noun that replaces a name.

Write the correct word to complete each sentence.

1. My (mother, Mother) writes poetry. <u>mother **(1 point)**</u>

2. She reads her poems to my (brother, Brother) and me.
   <u>brother **(1)**</u>

3. Sometimes she asks (dad, Dad) what he thinks, too.
   <u>Dad **(1)**</u>

4. Mom knows that (grandma, Grandma) has a good ear for rhythm.
   <u>Grandma **(1)**</u>

5. My little (sister, Sister) enjoys poems that rhyme.
   <u>sister **(1)**</u>

6. Grandfather Richards, my mother's (father, Father), writes
   funny limericks. <u>father **(1)**</u>

7. Does your (grandfather, Grandfather) write limericks?
   <u>grandfather **(1)**</u>

9. Sometimes (mom, Mom) wants me to help her
   choose the best word. <u>Mom **(1)**</u>

10. "Hey, (sis, Sis), please help me with this
    rhyme." <u>Sis **(1)**</u>

Hoop Season

Keeping Verbs in the Same Tense Be careful not to change verb
tenses unnecessarily in the middle of a paragraph.

**Write the correct verb forms that complete the
sentence in this description of a basketball game.**

Last night Dad and I (go, went) to a
basketball game. The fans (shout, shouted)
greetings to their favorite players, and some players
(waved, wave) back.

When the buzzer (rings, rang), the players
(charged, will charge) onto the court. The game (is,
was) slow for the first quarter. At halftime, people
(will crowd, crowded) the aisles and (munched, will
munch) popcorn.

In the second half, one guard suddenly
(passes, passed) the ball to the forward, who (pivots,
pivoted), (dribbled, will dribble) the ball, and
(ducked, will duck) under her opponent's
outstretched arms. She (hands, handed) the ball to
the center, who (slammed, slams) it through the
hoop. The fans (roar, roared)!

1. went **(1 point)**

2. shouted **(1)**

3. waved **(1)**

4. rang **(1)**

5. charged **(1)**

6. was **(1)**

7. crowded **(1)**

8. munched **(1)**

9. passed **(1)**

10. pivoted **(1)**

11. dribbled **(1)**

12. ducked **(1)**

13. handed **(1)**

14. slammed **(1)**

15. roared **(1)**

Assessment Tip: Total **15** Points

Name _____

Family Reunion

Using Capital Letters Correctly Capitalize a noun that names a particular person, place, or thing. Capitalize a word that takes the place of a name.

Use proofreading marks to correct the ten errors in punctuation and capitalization in these observations for a poem.

Example: every fall our Family has a reunion at harvest time!

Ten cars full of relatives turn at the Sign pointing to fox hollow. Their cars bounce into grandmas front yard and putter to a stop.

Everyone helps with the cooking. Aunt Marylou washes and cuts greens. One Cousin stirs batter for a huge pan of cornbread. The other Aunts help my mother prepare the tables. In the back, all the uncles gather around the barbecue and tease uncle Don. He and Dad always take charge of cooking the chicken and the ribs.

Cousins chase each other through the cornfield on this sunny october day. What a wonderful day we have?!

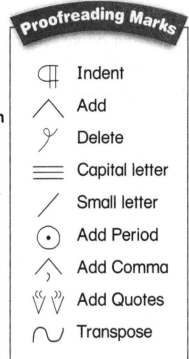

Proofreading Marks

⊓	Indent
∧	Add
ꝯ	Delete
＝	Capital letter
/	Small letter
⊙	Add Period
∧	Add Comma
＂ ＂	Add Quotes
∽	Transpose

Name _____

Planning a Poem

Put the most important ideas for your poem in the first column. If your poem tells a story, list the events. If your poem describes a person, place, thing, or memory, list its main features or actions. Then add details about each item and some of the exact words you'll use.

Topic: Answers will vary. _____

The mood I want to express: _____

Main Events or Features	Descriptive Details

Exact Words (sense words, adjectives, and so on)	Rhyme Words

Assessment Tip: Total **6** Points

Name _____

Words That Sound Like What They Mean

Read each sentence. Choose the best word to complete it, and write it on the blank. (1 point each**)**

1. At the picnic I enjoy a hot <u>sizzling</u> burger.

2. I drink fruit punch that is <u>fizzy</u> and cold.

3. We <u>crumple</u> the paper plates after we eat.

4. The pots and pans <u>rattle</u> as we wash them.

5. Later I walk on the beach and <u>scuff</u> the sand.

6. I like the rhythm of the waves as they <u>slosh</u> on to shore.

7. As I wade along the shore, I feel water <u>tickle</u> my feet.

8. Above my head, the sea gulls <u>squawk</u> at one another.

9. I <u>clap</u> my hands to make them fly away.

10. My sweatshirt keeps me warm so I don't <u>shiver</u>.

grumble
sizzling
scuff
tickle
snap
rattle
fizzy
musty
stomp
fluttering
whiny
clap
squawk
slippery
crumple
shrill
slosh
shiver

Write two sentences of your own. Use a word that sounds like what it means in each sentence. Use words from the box, or choose your own. (2 points each**)**

11. <u>Answers will vary.</u>

_____

_____

12. <u>Answers will vary.</u>

_____

_____

Name _____

Voices of the Revolution

After reading each selection, complete the chart below and on the next page to show what you discovered.

	And Then What Happened, Paul Revere?	Katie's Trunk	James Forten
What kind of writing is this selection an example of?	biography **(2 points)**	historical fiction **(2)**	biography **(2)**
Why was this story important to tell?	Paul Revere was a great American hero. It is important to tell his story so that people will remember him and his contributions. **(2)**	This story is important to tell because it helps readers understand that there were two sides to the American Revolutionary War, and that people on both sides suffered. **(2)**	James Forten's story is important to tell because it helps readers understand the contributions made by African-Americans before, during, and after the American Revolution. **(2)**
What character traits are revealed by the character's actions?	Paul Revere shows cleverness, courage, creativity, and intelligence. **(2)**	Katie shows fierce emotion, a strong sense of what is right and wrong, and a tendency to act without thinking. **(2)**	James Forten shows the ability to work hard, think for himself, and survive difficult challenges. **(2)**

Assessment Tip: Total **10** Points per selection and **2** Points for the final question

Name _____

Voices of the Revolution continued

	And Then What Happened, Paul Revere?	Katie's Trunk	James Forten
What details about colonial life did you learn from the selection?	I learned more about the kinds of jobs people did. **(2)**	I learned more about daily life and about what colonial homes were like. **(2)**	I learned about jobs aboard ships, and about what cities such as Philadelphia were like. **(2)**
What do you think the author's purpose for writing this selection was?	The author wanted to teach readers about Paul Revere's life and work and help them understand his many talents and skills. **(2)**	The author wanted to entertain readers with an exciting story, and also help them see that there were real people on both sides of the conflict. **(2)**	The author wanted to help readers understand the contributions of African-Americans, and inform them about an African American not many people know about. **(2)**

How did the selections in *Voices of the Revolution* increase your understanding of life in that period?

Possible response: I grew to understand how important the fight for independence

was in people's daily lives, and I learned that people had different points of view

about the war. **(2)**

Assessment Tip: Total **10** Points per selection and **2** Points for the final question

Name _____

Resisting Oppression

Use the words in the box to complete the paragraphs below.

The residents of America's thirteen <u>colonies **(1 point)**</u>
resented the new <u>taxes **(1)**</u> levied on them by
the British government. A group of citizens in the Boston area
formed a secret club to <u>oppose **(1)**</u> England's
method of governing America. The organization was known as
the Sons of Liberty, and every member was a
<u>Patriot **(1)**</u>. The group won a place in history
when its members dumped a <u>cargo **(1)**</u> of tea
into Boston Harbor to protest the tax on that commodity.

As it became clear that England would never allow the colonists
a voice in their own government, Americans began discussing the
possibility of <u>revolution **(1)**</u>. That kind of talk was
dangerous, though, so messages were carried secretly by
<u>express **(1)**</u> riders from one city to another. The
riders had to elude <u>sentries **(1)**</u> or they would be
deprived of their <u>liberty **(1)**</u>. The communications
network they established proved to be very valuable when war
finally broke out.

Choose one of the vocabulary words and write a sentence.

(1) _____

_____

Vocabulary

- revolution
- express
- cargo
- colonies
- oppose
- liberty
- Patriot
- sentries
- taxes

Name _____

Fact or Opinion?

Fill in the chart with facts or opinions from the pages indicated
in the first column. Where indicated, explain why the viewpoint
is a fact or an opinion.

Page	Statement	Fact or Opinion	Viewpoint Revealed
263	"Of all the busy people in Boston, Paul Revere would turn out to be one of the busiest."	Opinion	This statement shows that the author believes Paul Revere was busy all his life. She seems to be very impressed by him.
264	"In Boston there was always plenty to see." **(1 point)**	Opinion	The author seems to think Boston was a very interesting and engaging place to be. **(2)**
266	"You would think that with all Paul Revere did, he would make mistakes. But he always remembered to put spouts on his teapots... **(1)**	Fact	The author is amazed by Revere's abilities to do so much so well. She seems to think he was an exceptional individual. **(2)**
269	"He was back in Boston on the eleventh day, long before anyone expected him." **(1)**	Fact	Again, the author makes a statement that shows how impressive Revere's deeds were. **(2)**
275	"He did not stop to think that this might be the first battle of a war. His job was to move a trunk to safety, and that's what he did." **(1)**	Opinion and Fact	The author shows how dedicated Revere was to the cause of the Patriots. **(2)**

Assessment Tip: Total **12** Points

Name _____

When Did It Happen, Paul Revere?

The timeline below lists some important dates in Paul Revere's life. Answer the questions next to each date to help complete the timeline.

1735 — What is Boston like when Paul Revere is born?

There are 42 streets, 4,000 houses, 12 churches, 4 schools, many

horses and dogs, and about 15,000 people. There is plenty to see;

many ships coming and going, and street vendors. **(1 point)**

1756 — How does Revere respond when French soldiers and Indians attack the colonies?

He grabs his belongings and goes to Fort Henry on Lake George. **(1)**

1773 — On the night of December 16, Revere and the other Sons of Liberty are very busy in Boston Harbor. What are they doing?

They paint their faces, pretending to be Indians, and march on board

the British ships and dump the tea in the harbor. **(1)**

1776 — On the night of April 18, Revere is sent to Lexington and Concord. What happens on his Big Ride?

He forgets the cloth to cover the oars, leaves his spurs at home, is

chased by two British officers, is detained and questioned by a British

patrol, is let go without his horse, and arrives in Lexington on foot. **(1)**

1783 — By the end of the war, Revere is 48 years old. What does he do?

He goes back to silversmithing, opens a hardware store, sets up

a foundry, makes church bells, and sets up a copper rolling mill. **(1)**

1810 — What is Boston like now that Revere is 75 years old?

No one counts the streets, the horses, or the houses; everyone is busy

putting up new buildings and making the city bigger. **(1)**

Theme 3: **Voices of the Revolution**   197
Assessment Tip: Total **6** Points

Name _____

Viewing the Author

Read the passage. Then answer the questions on page 199.

Traitor or Hero?

How should Benedict Arnold be
remembered: as a traitor, or as a hero of the
American Revolution? I'm not sure this
question has a simple answer.

Arnold joined the Patriot militia in 1774.
After the Revolutionary War began in 1775, he
helped lead the capture of Fort Ticonderoga
from the British. Later that year, he led over a thousand soldiers into
Canada, was wounded in battle, and earned a promotion for bravery. In
October of 1777, he was again seriously wounded as he led his soldiers
against the forces of the British general Burgoyne. Arnold's courageous
leadership helped the Americans win one of their most important victories in
the war.

But in 1780, Arnold worked out a plan with the British to surrender an
important American military base in exchange for money. After his plan was
discovered, he escaped and joined the British army. Why did he do this?
Many historians believe that Arnold felt his country had treated him unfairly.
He was disappointed when he was passed over for a promotion. He was also
accused of being too easy on Americans who were loyal to the British. This
may have angered him.

The British never paid Arnold all the money he asked for. The land
they gave him in Canada was not useful to him. When Arnold died in 1801,
he had become poor, discouraged, and lonely, for he was a man few people
trusted. Arnold was a traitor, it is true. But we should not forget that he
performed several heroic acts that helped our nation win its independence.

Name _____

Viewing the Author continued

1. What is the viewpoint of the author of this passage? Sample answers shown.

   The author thinks Benedict Arnold was not just a traitor. He should also be

   remembered as a hero. **(2 points)**

2. Which sentences reveal the author's viewpoint?

   the first two sentences and the last two sentences **(2)**

   _____

3. What do you think the author's purpose is for writing this passage?

   The author wants to inform us about different sides of Benedict Arnold. **(2)**

   _____

4. Write a sentence from the passage that shows the author's opinion.

   "I'm not sure this question has a simple answer." **(2)**

   _____

5. Write a fact from the passage that helps to support the author's viewpoint.

   Arnold helped lead the capture of Fort Ticonderoga. **(2)**

   _____

6. Write a fact from the passage that
   might support a different
   viewpoint about the subject.
   In 1780, Arnold worked out a plan
   with the British to surrender an
   important American military base.
   (2)

   _____

   _____

Name _____

No Apostrophes!

Your school is putting on a play of _And Then What Happened, Paul Revere?_ You're sending an e-mail to the script writer, but the apostrophe (') on the computer doesn't work! Change each contraction or possessive to its longer form. Write P for possessive or C for contraction in each box.

1. Paul makes a squirrel's silver collar.

   Paul makes a silver collar of a squirrel. **(1 point)** _____ | P | **(1)**

2. The writing's sloppy in the letters Paul writes.

   The writing is sloppy in the letters Paul writes. **(1)** _____ | C | **(1)**

3. Paul rings the church bells at a moment's notice.

   Paul rings the church bells at the notice of a moment. **(1)** _____ | P | **(1)**

4. The English are taxing tea, glass, and printers' inks.

   The English are taxing tea, glass, and the inks of printers. **(1)** | P | **(1)**

5. Paul doesn't miss a chance to help the Sons of Liberty.

   Paul does not miss a chance to help the Sons of Liberty. **(1)** | C | **(1)**

6. A messenger's job is to travel from place to place on horseback.

   The job of a messenger is to travel from place to place on horseback. **(1)** | P | **(1)**

7. Cloth to cover the oars isn't all Paul leaves behind.

   Cloth to cover the oars is not all Paul leaves behind. **(1)** _____ | C | **(1)**

8. He goes back to rescue the Patriots' papers.

   He goes back to rescue the papers of the Patriots. **(1)** _____ | P | **(1)**

Assessment Tip: Total **16** Points

Name _____

Final /ər/

The **schwa sound** is a weak vowel sound that is often found in an unstressed syllable. It is shown as /ə/. When you hear the final /ər/ sound in words of more than one syllable, think of the patterns *er*, *or*, and *ar*:

/ər/ ang**er**, act**or**, pill**ar**

Write each Spelling Word under the pattern that spells its final /ər/ sound. Order of answers for each category may vary.

Spelling Words

1. theater
2. actor
3. mirror
4. powder
5. humor
6. anger
7. banner
8. pillar
9. major
10. thunder
11. flavor
12. finger
13. mayor
14. polar
15. clover
16. burglar
17. tractor
18. matter
19. lunar
20. quarter

er

theater **(1 point)**

powder **(1)**

anger **(1)**

banner **(1)**

thunder **(1)**

finger **(1)**

clover **(1)**

matter **(1)**

quarter **(1)**

or

actor **(1)**

mirror **(1)**

humor **(1)**

major **(1)**

flavor **(1)**

mayor **(1)**

tractor **(1)**

ar

pillar **(1)**

polar **(1)**

burglar **(1)**

lunar **(1)**

Theme 3: **Voices of the Revolution**   201
Assessment Tip: Total **20** Points

Name _____

Spelling Spree

Find a Rhyme For each sentence write a Spelling Word
that rhymes with the underlined word and makes sense.

1. Do me a <u>favor</u> and pick a different _____ of ice cream.
2. I <u>wonder</u> if we'll hear _____ during the rainstorm.
3. The town paved <u>over</u> a field of _____.
4. The butler hung a colorful _____ outside the <u>manor</u>.
5. Put the _____ in the coin <u>sorter</u>.
6. They hope to run the _____ station on <u>solar</u> power.
7. The _____ was a <u>factor</u> in the movie's success.

1. flavor **(1 point)**
2. thunder **(1)**
3. clover **(1)**
4. banner **(1)**
5. quarter **(1)**
6. polar **(1)**
7. actor **(1)**

Puzzle Play Write the Spelling Word that fits each clue. Then
write the circled letters in order below. **(1 point each)**

8. a farm machine
9. a pointer or a pinky
10. fury
11. a column
12. a thief
13. a surface that reflects
14. place for movies
15. person in charge of a city

t	r	a	c	(t)	o	r
	f	i	n	g	(e)	r
	(a)	n	g	e	r
	(p)	i	l	l	a	r
b	u	r	g	l	(a)	r
	m	i	r	r	o	(r)
t	h	e	a	(t)	e	r
	m	a	(y)	o	r

Mystery Words: a t e a p a r t y

Spelling Words

1. theater
2. actor
3. mirror
4. powder
5. humor
6. anger
7. banner
8. pillar
9. major
10. thunder
11. flavor
12. finger
13. mayor
14. polar
15. clover
16. burglar
17. tractor
18. matter
19. lunar
20. quarter

Assessment Tip: Total **15** Points

Name _____

Proofreading and Writing

Proofreading Circle the five misspelled Spelling Words in this notice to British troops. Then write each word correctly.

April 16, 1775

From Boston Headquarters:

We are planning a major march into the countryside on the evening of the 18th. The current lunor phase will give us a full moon, so there will be plenty of light. If all goes well, we will surprise the rebels and take their supplies of guns and powdur. This mater should be kept secret, of course. Stay calm, and react to any unpleasant situations with humer rather than anger. More details will follow.

1. major **(1 point)**
2. lunar **(1)**
3. powder **(1)**
4. matter **(1)**
5. humor **(1)**

Spelling Words

1. theater
2. actor
3. mirror
4. powder
5. humor
6. anger
7. banner
8. pillar
9. major
10. thunder
11. flavor
12. finger
13. mayor
14. polar
15. clover
16. burglar
17. tractor
18. matter
19. lunar
20. quarter

✏️ **Write Interview Questions** If you could interview Paul Revere, what questions would you ask him? Would you like to know more about his work as a silversmith or details of his famous ride?

On a separate piece of paper, write some questions that you would like to ask this famous patriot about his life and the historical events in which he took part. Use Spelling Words from the list.

Responses will vary. **(5)**

Name _____

Synonym Switch

Find a synonym in the box for each underlined word.
Rewrite the sentences using the synonyms.

1. In Boston Harbor, ships constantly <u>came</u> and <u>left</u>.
   In Boston Harbor, ships constantly arrived and departed.

   (2 points)

2. Paul <u>found</u> that money could be <u>made</u> in many ways.
   Paul discovered that money could be earned in many

   ways. **(2)**

3. The men <u>hauled</u> the chests to the deck and <u>tossed</u> the tea
   overboard.
   The men dragged the chests to the deck and threw the tea

   overboard. **(2)**

4. Paul <u>slipped</u> past the sentries and <u>dashed</u> through the snow.
   Paul sneaked past the sentries and hurried through the

   snow. **(2)**

5. Paul <u>beat</u> on doors in Lexington and <u>aroused</u> the citizens.
   Paul pounded on doors in Lexington and woke the

   citizens. **(2)**

204   Theme 3: **Voices of the Revolution**
Assessment Tip: Total **10** Points

Where's Your House, Paul Revere?

Subject-Verb Agreement A verb must agree in number with its subject. In the present tense, add *-s* or *-es* to the verb if the subject is singular. Do not add *-s* or *-es* if the subject is plural or if the subject is *I* or *you*. If you are using *be* or *have* as helping verbs, use the form that agrees with the subject in number.

Complete each sentence with the present-tense form of the verb in parentheses that agrees with the subject in number.

1. We __are **(1 point)**__ visiting Paul Revere's house in Boston. (be)

2. My cousin __likes **(1)**__ the silver teapot on display. (like)

3. I __see **(1)**__ tankards Paul Revere made. (see)

4. A 900-pound bell __stands **(1)**__ in the courtyard of the Revere house. (stand)

5. The silver cup and tray __shine **(1)**__ brightly. (shine)

6. You __walk **(1)**__ to the Old North Church. (walk)

7. She __is **(1)**__ gazing at the church steeple where the lanterns hung. (be)

8. I __imagine **(1)**__ Revere's midnight ride to Lexington. (imagine)

9. Tourists __walk **(1)**__ the Freedom Trail in Boston. (walk)

10. I __have **(1)**__ learned about American patriots. (have)

Assessment Tip: Total **10** Points

What Was Your Ride Like, Paul Revere?

Regular and Irregular Verbs To form the past tense of regular verbs, add *-ed* to the verb. Irregular verbs have special forms for the past tense. Do not add *-ed* to irregular verbs.

Tracy and Kim have written an interview to perform in history class. To enjoy the interview, fill in the correct past-tense forms of the verbs in parentheses. You may have to check irregular verbs in your dictionary.

Reporter: We are on the scene with the famous Patriot Paul Revere. Mr. Revere, you have returned from an important mission. What was it like on that ride, sir?

Paul Revere: My midnight ride <u>was **(1 point)**</u> (be) exciting. I <u>rode **(1)**</u> (ride) as fast as I <u>could **(1)**</u> (can)! I don't think I have ever <u>ridden **(1)**</u> (ride) so fast before!

Reporter: We have heard that you <u>forgot **(1)**</u> (forget) your spurs. Is that true?

Paul Revere: Yes, I <u>did **(1)**</u> (do), but my faithful dog <u>brought **(1)**</u> (bring) them to me.

Reporter: You also <u>rowed **(1)**</u> (row) across the river, right?

Paul Revere: I <u>ran **(1)**</u> (run) as fast as I could, too, and I <u>warned **(1)**</u> (warn) the people about the British.

Reporter: Paul Revere, American Patriot, your country is grateful.

Assessment Tip: Total **10** Points

Name _____

What Did You See, Shirley Jensen?

Choosing the Correct Verb Form It is important for a writer to choose the correct form of a verb. For irregular verbs, you may have to check your dictionary.

Shirley keeps a journal on her computer. She recently took a trip to Boston and wants to write an essay about her experience. To get started, she has printed out her journal entries. Proofread the journal entry below and circle the incorrect verb forms. Then write the correct form above the error. (1 point each)

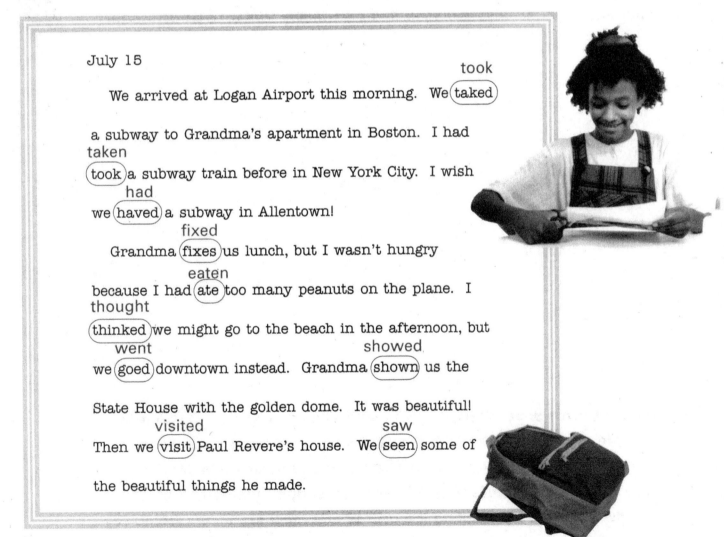

July 15

We arrived at Logan Airport this morning. We (taked)   *took*

a subway to Grandma's apartment in Boston. I had
(took) a subway train before in New York City. I wish   *taken*

we (haved) a subway in Allentown!   *had*

Grandma (fixes) us lunch, but I wasn't hungry   *fixed*

because I had (ate) too many peanuts on the plane. I   *eaten*

(thinked) we might go to the beach in the afternoon, but   *thought*

we (goed) downtown instead. Grandma (shown) us the   *went*   *showed*

State House with the golden dome. It was beautiful!

Then we (visit) Paul Revere's house. We (seen) some of   *visited*   *saw*

the beautiful things he made.

Name _____

Writing a Character Sketch

And Then What Happened, Paul Revere? gives many details about Paul
Revere, a hero of the American Revolution. These details help you
understand what he did and what kind of person he was. Using vivid
details in your writing can help bring a real person like Paul Revere or a
story character to life.

A **character sketch** is a written profile that describes how a real
person or a story character looks, acts, thinks, and feels.

**Choose a real person or a story character from another selection you
have read whom you think would make a good subject for a
character sketch. Then use the web to brainstorm details about the
character's physical appearance and personality traits. (2 points each)**

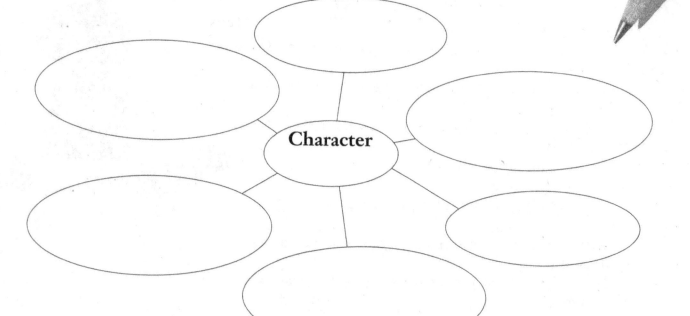

**On a separate sheet of paper, write your character sketch. Begin with
a quote or an anecdote about the character. Then write a sentence
that summarizes his or her most significant character traits. Next,
give two or three details from the web that support your summary.
Finally, conclude by restating the character's most significant traits. (2)**

Assessment Tip: Total **14** Points

Name _____

Using Exact Nouns and Verbs

Which noun, *lights* or *chandeliers*, is more exact? Which verb, *galloped* or
rode, is more exact? A good writer avoids using vague nouns and verbs.
Exact nouns and verbs like *chandeliers* and *galloped* can make your writing
clearer and help readers create a more vivid mental picture of the people,
places, and events that you describe.

**One fifth-grader drafted these sentences for a character sketch about
Paul Revere. Can you help her make her writing clearer and more
vivid? Rewrite each sentence on the lines, replacing the underlined
vague nouns and verbs with more exact ones from the list below.**

More Exact Nouns and Verbs

crafted	careers
hardware store	colonists
opened	warned
tea	silver
pursued	dumped

1. Throughout his life, Paul Revere <u>did</u> many different <u>things</u>.
   Throughout his life, Paul Revere pursued many different careers. **(2 points)**

   _____

2. He <u>made</u> pitchers, candlesticks, and buckles from <u>metal</u>.
   He crafted pitchers, candlesticks, and buckles from silver. **(2)**

   _____

3. With other patriots, he disguised himself as an Indian, boarded a
   British ship, and <u>put</u> <u>stuff</u> into Boston Harbor.
   With other patriots, he disguised himself as an Indian, boarded a British ship,

   and dumped tea into Boston Harbor.**(2)**

4. He became a hero when he <u>told</u> <u>people</u> that British troops were coming.
   He became a hero when he warned colonists that British troops were coming.**(2)**

   _____

Name _____

Revising Your Story

**Reread your story. Put a checkmark in the box for each sentence that describes
your paper. Use this page to help you revise.**

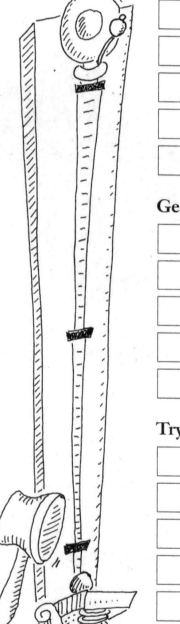

Rings the Bell

☐ My setting, characters, and plot are well developed.

☐ The beginning, middle, and end are clear. Events are in order.

☐ My writing creates a particular mood for my story.

☐ Details, exact words, and dialogue bring my story to life.

☐ Sentences flow smoothly. There are very few mistakes.

Getting Stronger

☐ The setting, characters, and plot could be more interesting.

☐ Parts of the story are missing. Some events are out of order.

☐ My story does not sound the way I want it to.

☐ More details, exact words, and dialogue are needed.

☐ Sentences flow smoothly. There are a few mistakes.

Try Harder

☐ There is no setting or plot. My characters are flat.

☐ There is no beginning or ending. The order is confusing.

☐ You can't hear my voice. My story has no particular mood.

☐ There are no details or exact words. I didn't use dialogue.

☐ Sentences are short or unclear, with many mistakes.

Name _____

Using Exact Verbs

Replace each underlined verb. Circle the letter of the verb that best completes each sentence. (1 point each)

1. Nina <u>rearranged</u> the cards in the deck.

   a. moved   b. mixed   (c.) shuffled   d. wrinkled

2. "<u>Have</u> one card," she said to Ted. "Then put it back into the deck."

   a. Replace   (b.) Remove   c. Repair   d. Deliver

3. "Is this your card?" she asked, <u>showing</u> the Queen of Hearts.

   (a.) flashing   b. flushing   c. hiding   d. presenting

4. Ted <u>moved</u> his head sadly. "No, it's not my card," he said.

   a. rotated   b. turned   c. stiffened   (d.) shook

5. "Oh goodness," Nina said. "I've <u>done it</u> again."

   a. smiled   (b.) misjudged   c. blundered   d. coughed

6. Then Nina's hand <u>went</u> behind her ear and pulled out a card.

   a. fell   (b.) darted   c. skipped   d. grasped

7. "That's my card," Ted <u>said</u>. "The deuce of clubs!"

   a. mentioned   b. noted   (c.) exclaimed   d. whispered

8. "Thank you very much," Nina said. She bowed to her audience and <u>ran</u> off the stage.

   (a.) scampered   b. slinked   c. wriggled   d. skipped

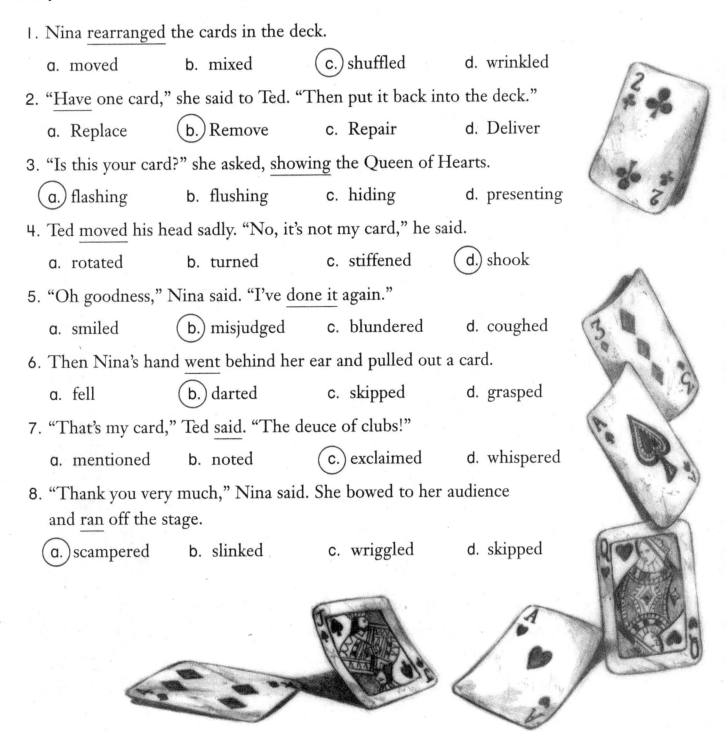

Assessment Tip: Total **8** Points

Spelling Words

Words Often Misspelled Look for familiar spelling patterns to help you remember how to spell the Spelling Words on this page. Think carefully about the parts that you find hard to spell in each word.

Write the missing letters in the Spelling Words below.

1. happ <u>i</u> ly **(1 point)**

2. min <u>u</u> t <u>e</u> **(1)**

3. b <u>e</u> a <u>u</u> t <u>i</u> ful **(1)**

4. usua <u>l</u> <u>l</u> y **(1)**

5. inst <u>e</u> a <u>d</u> **(1)**

6. stre <u>t</u> c <u>h</u> **(1)**

7. l <u>y</u> ing **(1)**

8. e <u>x</u> c <u>ite</u> **(1)**

9. mil <u>l</u> i <u>meter</u> **(1)**

10. d <u>i</u> v <u>i</u> d <u>e</u> **(1)**

11. unt <u>i</u> l **(1)**

12. wri <u>t</u> i <u>ng</u> **(1)**

13. tr <u>i</u> e <u>d</u> **(1)**

14. b <u>e</u> f <u>o</u> r <u>e</u> **(1)**

15. <u>S</u> at <u>u</u> r <u>day</u> **(1)**

Study List On a separate piece of paper, write each Spelling Word. Check your spelling against the words on the list.
Order of words may vary.

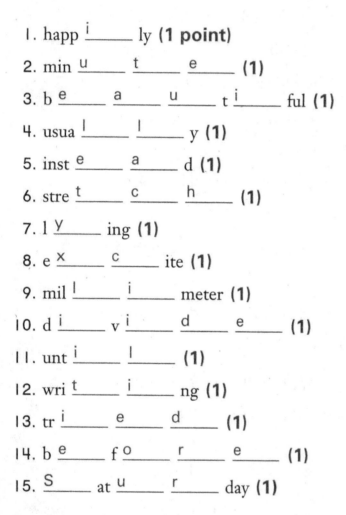

Spelling Words

1. happily
2. minute
3. beautiful
4. usually
5. instead
6. stretch
7. lying
8. excite
9. millimeter
10. divide
11. until
12. writing
13. tried
14. before
15. Saturday

Assessment Tip: Total **15** Points

Name _____

Spelling Spree

Phrase Fillers Write the Spelling Word that best completes each phrase.

1. a _____ and true method
2. to yawn and _____
3. wait a _____
4. _____ down for a nap
5. to _____ into two pieces
6. dinner comes _____ dessert
7. _____ a letter

<table>
<tr><td>1. tried (1 point)</td><td>5. divide (1)</td></tr>
<tr><td>2. stretch (1)</td><td>6. before (1)</td></tr>
<tr><td>3. minute (1)</td><td>7. writing (1)</td></tr>
<tr><td>4. lying (1)</td><td></td></tr>
</table>

Syllable Scramble Rearrange the syllables to write a Spelling Word. One syllable in each item is extra.

<table>
<tr><td>8. til un till</td><td>8. until (1)</td></tr>
<tr><td>9. ur date day Sat</td><td>9. Saturday (1)</td></tr>
<tr><td>10. cite ite ex</td><td>10. excite (1)</td></tr>
<tr><td>11. ly u al fer su</td><td>11. usually (1)</td></tr>
<tr><td>12. pi hap an ly</td><td>12. happily (1)</td></tr>
<tr><td>13. in ted stead</td><td>13. instead (1)</td></tr>
<tr><td>14. ti ness ful beau</td><td>14. beautiful (1)</td></tr>
<tr><td>15. mil time ter li me</td><td>15. millimeter (1)</td></tr>
</table>

Spelling Words

1. happily
2. minute
3. beautiful
4. usually
5. instead
6. stretch
7. lying
8. excite
9. millimeter
10. divide
11. until
12. writing
13. tried
14. before
15. Saturday

Name _____

Proofreading and Writing

Proofreading Circle the five misspelled Spelling Words in this open letter. Then write each word correctly.

Fellow Countrymen:

I am (riting) these words to urge you all to action. This land cannot spend another (minut) under the tyrannical rule of the British King! We have (tride) to plead and reason with him, but he will not listen. Now, (insted) of talking, we must fight! If we do, it will not be long before we are living (hapilly) in our own nation. Join the struggle for liberty now!

1. happily
2. minute
3. beautiful
4. usually
5. instead
6. stretch
7. lying
8. excite
9. millimeter
10. divide
11. until
12. writing
13. tried
14. before
15. Saturday

1. writing **(1 point)**
2. minute **(1)**
3. tried **(1)**
4. instead **(1)**
5. happily **(1)**

Slogan Writing Pick three Spelling Words. Then, with each one, write a slogan (such as "Don't Tread on Me" or "Liberty or Death") that could have been used during the Revolutionary War. Responses will vary. **(5)**

Assessment Tip: Total **10** Points

Name _____

Some Talk of Revolution

Answer each of the following questions by writing a vocabulary word.

1. Which word means "right" or "fair"?
   just **(1 point)** _____

2. Which word names individuals fighting against their government? rebels **(1)** _____

3. Which word means "giving weapons to"?
   arming **(1)** _____

4. Which word means "practicing for battle"?
   drilling **(1)** _____

5. Which word is a synonym for *nervous*?
   skittish **(1)** _____

6. Which word means "looked"?
   peered **(1)** _____

7. Which word is an antonym for *meek*?
   fierce **(1)** _____

8. Which word means "a brief battle"?
   skirmish **(1)** _____

9. Which word is a synonym for *relatives*?
   kin **(1)** _____

Write a different question using one of the vocabulary words.

(1) _____

_____

Name _____

Why Did It Happen?

Fill in the columns where indicated with the cause or the effect of the events included in the chart.

Causes	Effects
Fights have broken out in the colonies, and rebels have called for independence from British rule. **(2)**	The uneasiness and fighting make Katie's family feel skittish, nervous, and worried.
Friends and neighbors disagree about whether to fight or be loyal to British rule. **(2)**	The family has lost friends and neighbors.
Armed rebels come to Katie's home.	The family goes to the woods to hide. **(2)**
Katie feels that it is not just for their neighbors to break into their house and ruin their things.	Katie rushes back to the house to protect it. **(2)**
Katie becomes afraid when she hears the rebels tearing off the knocker on the door. **(2)**	Katie hides inside her mother's wedding trunk.
When John Warren searches the trunk and discovers Katie, he calls the rebels away and leaves the lid open so she can breathe.	Katie realizes that goodness still exists in people, despite the conflicts they might have with each other. **(2)**

Assessment Tip: Total **12** Points

Name _____

In the Characters' Words

Read the characters' words in the left column. In the right column, write why each character said what he or she did.

What the Character Said	Why the Character Said It
Mama: "It makes me as skittish as a newborn calf."	There was talk of war with England. Neighbors were no longer speaking. **(2 points)**
Papa: "Get your mother! Hide in the woods."	The rebels were coming to Katie's house and the family had to hide. **(2)**
Katie: "It was not right. It was not just. It was not fair."	Katie became angry when she thought about her family's rebel neighbors ruining their things. **(2)**
The rebels: "This'll be fine pickings!"	The house was full of English goods, and the rebels were trying to steal the valuables to sell for arms. **(2)**
John Warren: "Out! The Tories are coming. Back to the road! Hurry!"	John Warren found Katie in the trunk and he didn't want her to get hurt by the rebels, so he made up a lie. **(2)**
Katie: "He'd left one seam of goodness there, and we were all tied to it."	John Warren proved there was goodness left in him, and Katie felt there was some good in everyone. **(2)**

Assessment Tip: Total **12** Points

Name _____

Making Connections

Read the story. Then complete the activity on page 219.

A Dangerous Day

My name is Margaret Tompkins. I work as a nurse in a field hospital here in Virginia. When my brother enlisted as a soldier in the Continental army, I, too, wanted to join and help the cause. I decided to become a nurse. I came to this area three months ago when my brother's company was sent here.

For the past few hours, our soldiers have been involved in a fierce battle. After almost ten hours of fighting, they are exhausted and very hungry. Some of the wounded have been brought to the hospital, where the other nurses and I have been treating them. It is hard, heartbreaking work.

It is now just past three in the afternoon. Over the noise, I suddenly hear my brother's voice calling "Margaret!" I grab a medical bag and run out onto the field. When I reach James, he is sitting next to a cannon, holding his left shoulder.

"What has happened?" I ask him.

"The cannon recoiled and twisted my shoulder out of its socket," he tells me. I tell James I will lead him to the hospital so he can be treated. He shakes his head. "I can't leave here," he says. "Someone has to fire the cannon."

I look around and realize that, for the moment, no one else is nearby. Finally I say, "James, you cannot fire a cannon with a dislocated shoulder. You go. I have watched cannons being fired. I'll take a turn here." He goes.

I feel afraid. But I prepare the cannon. Here is a chance to do more to win the war than just unroll bandages.

Name _____

Making Connections continued

Complete the cause-effect chain to show what caused the events described on page 218, and what happened as a result. Sample answers shown.

Causes	Effects
Margaret wants to help the Patriot effort.	Margaret becomes a nurse. **(2 points)**
Margaret's brother's company is sent to Virginia. **(2)**	Margaret travels to Virginia to work in a field hospital and be near him.
The cannon James is firing recoils into him. **(2)**	James's shoulder is dislocated.
James refuses to get his shoulder treated because he is the only soldier at the post.	Margaret tells him she will fire the cannon and sends him to the hospital. **(2)**
Margaret wants to help the Patriots win the war. **(2)**	Margaret prepares the cannon even though she feels afraid.

Name _____

Signalling Syllables

**Rewrite each underlined word, adding slashes between its syllables.
Then write a definition of the word.** Sample answers shown.

1. The family usually sat and talked with visitors in the parlor.
   par/lor **(1 point)**; a room for entertaining visitors **(1)**

2. Katie's mother is skittish because of the fighting in the area.
   skit/tish **(1)**; nervous, uneasy **(1)**

3. Dragonflies would land briefly on the rocks before flying away again.
   drag/on/flies **(1)**; large flying insects **(1)**

4. As she hid in the trunk, Katie heard faraway voices and footsteps.
   far/a/way **(1)**; distant **(1)**

5. The incident was just a skirmish, not a major battle.
   skir/mish **(1)**; a minor conflict **(1)**

6. A large horse went thudding by on the road.
   thud/ding **(1)**; making a heavy, dull sound **(1)**

220   Theme 3: **Voices of the Revolution**
Assessment Tip: Total **12** Points

Name _____

VCCV and VCV Patterns

A **syllable** is a word part with one vowel sound. To spell a two-syllable word, divide the word into syllables. Divide a VCCV word between the consonants. Divide a VCV word before or after the consonant. Look for spelling patterns you have learned, and spell the word by syllables.

VC | CV	VC | CV
ar | rive	**par | lor**

VC | V	V | CV
val | ue	**a | ware**
clos | et	**be | have**

Write each Spelling Word under the heading that tells how it is divided. Order of answers for each category may vary.

1. equal
2. parlor
3. collect
4. closet
5. perhaps
6. wedding
7. rapid
8. value
9. arrive
10. behave
11. shoulder
12. novel
13. tulip
14. sorrow
15. vanish
16. essay
17. publish
18. aware
19. subject
20. prefer

VC | CV

parlor **(1 point)**

collect **(1)**

perhaps **(1)**

wedding **(1)**

arrive **(1)**

shoulder **(1)**

sorrow **(1)**

essay **(1)**

publish **(1)**

subject **(1)**

VC | V

closet **(1)**

rapid **(1)**

value **(1)**

novel **(1)**

vanish **(1)**

V | CV

equal **(1)**

behave **(1)**

tulip **(1)**

aware **(1)**

prefer **(1)**

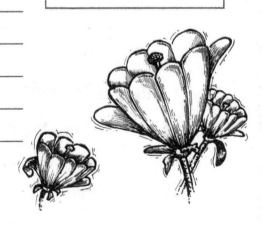

Name _____

Spelling Spree

Syllable Match Match each of the following syllables with one of the numbered syllables to create Spelling Words. Then write the words on the blanks provided.

ar	qual	have	par	a
et	wed	pre	lish	el

1. **nov**   novel **(1 point)**

2. **lor**   parlor **(1)**

3. **fer**   prefer **(1)**

4. **clos**   closet **(1)**

5. **e**   equal **(1)**

6. **ding**   wedding **(1)**

7. **be**   behave **(1)**

8. **ware**   aware **(1)**

9. **rive**   arrive **(1)**

10. **pub**   publish **(1)**

The Third Word Write the Spelling Word that belongs with each group.

11. sadness, grief, sorrow **(1)**

12. possibly, maybe, perhaps **(1)**

13. worth, price, value **(1)**

14. gather, accumulate, collect **(1)**

15. fast, speedy, rapid **(1)**

16. rose, daffodil, tulip **(1)**

17. topic, field, subject **(1)**

18. paper, report, essay **(1)**

19. wrist, elbow, shoulder **(1)**

20. fade, disappear, vanish **(1)**

Spelling Words

1. equal
2. parlor
3. collect
4. closet
5. perhaps
6. wedding
7. rapid
8. value
9. arrive
10. behave
11. shoulder
12. novel
13. tulip
14. sorrow
15. vanish
16. essay
17. publish
18. aware
19. subject
20. prefer

Assessment Tip: Total **20** Points

Name _____

Proofreading and Writing

Proofreading Circle the five misspelled Spelling Words in this speech. Then write each word correctly.

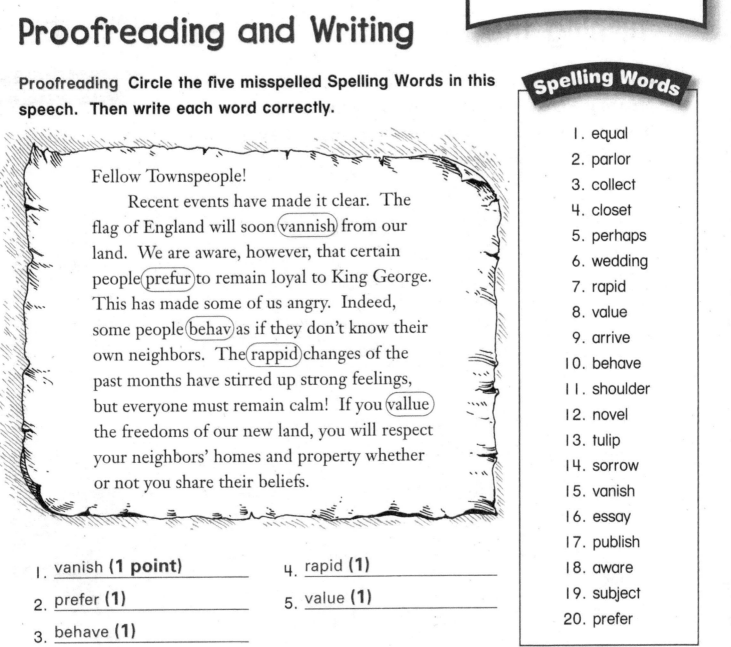

Fellow Townspeople!

Recent events have made it clear. The flag of England will soon (vannish) from our land. We are aware, however, that certain people (prefur) to remain loyal to King George. This has made some of us angry. Indeed, some people (behav) as if they don't know their own neighbors. The (rappid) changes of the past months have stirred up strong feelings, but everyone must remain calm! If you (vallue) the freedoms of our new land, you will respect your neighbors' homes and property whether or not you share their beliefs.

Spelling Words

1. equal
2. parlor
3. collect
4. closet
5. perhaps
6. wedding
7. rapid
8. value
9. arrive
10. behave
11. shoulder
12. novel
13. tulip
14. sorrow
15. vanish
16. essay
17. publish
18. aware
19. subject
20. prefer

1. vanish **(1 point)**

2. prefer **(1)**

3. behave **(1)**

4. rapid **(1)**

5. value **(1)**

▬▬▬ **Write a Bulletin-Board Notice** You want your classmates to join you in some activity, perhaps organizing a pep rally or raising money for disaster relief or some other worthy cause. How will you get their attention?

On a separate piece of paper, write a notice to tack up on a school bulletin board giving reasons why students should join you in the activity. Responses will vary. **(5)**

Theme 3: **Voices of the Revolution** 223
Assessment Tip: Total **10** Points

Name _____

Turning the Key

Use the spelling table/pronunciation key to figure out how to
pronounce the underlined words. Then find a word in the
box with the same vowel sound as the underlined word, and
write it after the sentence.

Vocabulary

meant

steer

blood

took

town

flour

Sounds	Spellings	Sample Words
/ĕ/	e, ea	shed, breath
/î/	ea, ee, ie, e	dear, deer, pier, mere
/ŭ/	o, u, ou, oo	cut, rough, flood
/o͝o/	u, oo, o	full, book, wolf
/ou/	ou, ow	about, crown

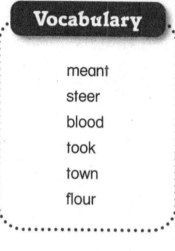

1. <u>Crouched</u> in the underbrush, I felt like an animal in a trap.
   flour or town **(2 points)**
   _____

2. In a <u>fierce</u> whisper, Mama was trying to call me back.
   steer **(2)**
   _____

3. The men ripped the knocker off the <u>wood</u>.
   took **(2)**
   _____

4. The rustle of the clothing in the trunk <u>drowned</u> their words.
   town or flour **(2)**
   _____

5. I could hear the <u>drums</u> of the rebels who were marching in
   town.
   blood **(2)**
   _____

6. A sudden <u>thread</u> of a song ran through my head.
   meant **(2)**
   _____

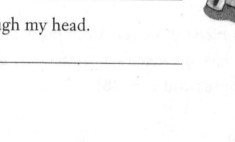

Name _____

Katie's Adventure

Verb Phrases with *have* Many verb phrases begin with a form of *have*, *has*, or *had*. Use *has* with singular subjects. Use *have* with plural subjects or with *I* or *you*. Use *had* with either singular subjects or plural subjects.

Underline the verb phrase in the following sentences.

1. Katie and her family <u>had been friends</u> with their neighbors before the revolution. **(1 point)**

2. Political differences now <u>have come</u> between them. **(1)**

3. It <u>has been</u> difficult for everyone. **(1)**

4. The rebels <u>have entered</u> the house. **(1)**

5. Katie <u>has hidden</u> in a trunk. **(1)**

Fill in the correct form of the verbs in parentheses to complete the following sentences.

6. They have <u>broken **(1)**</u> (break) a precious teapot.

7. It has <u>been **(1)**</u> (be) a trying time for the family.

8. I have <u>enjoyed **(1)**</u> (enjoy) reading the story about British loyalists.

9. You have <u>made **(1)**</u> (make) me think.

10. Mr. Roby had <u>hoped **(1)**</u> (hope) the class would like the story.

Name _____

Let Us Learn About Lexington

teach, learn; let, leave; sit, set; can, may Some pairs of verbs can be confusing. The meanings of these verbs are related but different. Study the definitions carefully.

teach—to instruct   let—to allow

learn—to be instructed   leave—to go away

sit—to rest or stay in one place   can—to have the ability to

set—to put   may—to have permission

Choose between the two verbs in parentheses to correctly complete each sentence.

1. We will <u>learn **(1 point)**</u> (teach, learn) about the American Revolution.

2. Ms. Amata will <u>teach **(1)**</u> (teach, learn) us about the Tories.

3. In Lexington, our class <u>can **(1)**</u> (can, may) see a statue of a Minuteman.

4. You <u>may **(1)**</u> (can, may) take my picture beside the statue.

5. In Boston, we <u>can **(1)**</u> (can, may) see the harbor where the rebels dumped the tea.

6. We will <u>sit **(1)**</u> (sit, set) on a bench at the harbor.

7. I'll <u>set **(1)**</u> (sit, set) my camera on the bench.

8. <u>May **(1)**</u> (Can, May) I borrow your history book?

9. My teacher <u>lets **(1)**</u> (lets, leaves) me ask many questions.

10. They will <u>leave **(1)**</u> (let, leave) before lunch.

Assessment Tip: Total **10** Points

Name _____

Uncle Warren's Trunk

Choosing the Correct Verb Michael is writing a letter to his cousin, but he is uncertain about the correct verb to use. Choose the correct verbs from the list to fill in the blanks.

teach
learn
let
leave
sit
set
can
may

Dear Kenya,

    I read a story about a girl who had to hide in a trunk. It reminded me of the trunk we saw in Uncle Warren's attic. Do you remember? I talked to Uncle Warren on Sunday, and he said that we __may **(1 point)**__ open it next time we visit. I hope we find a Revolutionary War sword inside! If we do, we __can **(1)**__ try to find out who owned it. We would __learn **(1)**__ a lot about history that way. Uncle Warren doesn't think we will find anything that old, but he said he will __teach **(1)**__ us about the history of our family.

    __Can **(1)**__ you come next Saturday? If not, will your parents __let **(1)**__ you come the following Saturday? If you __leave **(1)**__ your house before noon, we __can **(1)**__ have lunch. I will __sit **(1)__ on the porch and wait for you. I better __set **(1)**__ down my pen now and turn out the light.

              Your cousin,

              Michael

Name _____

Writing a Friendly Letter

Katie Gray in *Katie's Trunk* lived in the 1700s during the Revolutionary War — long before the invention of either the telephone or the computer. If she wanted to share her experience of hiding in the trunk, Katie could not have called a friend or sent an e-mail message. However, she might have written a friendly letter.

A **friendly letter** is a letter that you write to a friend to share news about your life.

Use this page to help you plan and organize a friendly letter. Either write to a friend of yours, or write a letter that Katie might have written to a friend. Use a separate sheet of paper, and follow these steps: (2 points each)

1. Write a **heading** (your address and the date) in the upper right corner.
2. Write a **greeting** (*Dear* and the person's name followed by a comma) at the left margin.
3. Write the **body** of your letter below the greeting. Begin by writing something that demonstrates you care about your friend. Include your personal thoughts, feelings, or news. Make sure to use a friendly tone and informal language. At the end of the letter, ask your friend to write back soon.
4. Write an informal **closing** such as *Love* or *Your friend* followed by a comma in the lower right corner.
5. Sign your name under the closing.

> Heading
> _____
> _____
> _____
> Greeting _____
> Body
> _____
> _____
> _____
> _____
> _____
> _____
> Closing _____
> Signature _____
> _____

When your friendly letter is finished, address an envelope and mail it or share it with a classmate.

Assessment Tip: Total **10** Points

Name _____

Voice

Every writer has a **voice**, or a unique way of expressing himself or herself. A writer's voice helps reveal what he or she is like as a person. You can sometimes also "hear" a narrator's or a character's voice when you read a work of literature. For example, listen for Mama's voice as you read this sentence from *Katie's Trunk:* "Tea! In the harbor! Wasting God's good food."

    You can strengthen your own writing voice when you write by showing more of what you think and feel, and by including expressions you commonly use when speaking, such as *No way!* or *I'm psyched* or *You've got to be kidding.*

On the lines below, write ten expressions that you commonly use when speaking.

My Common Expressions

(1 point) _____

(expression of fear)

(1) _____

(expression of surprise)

(1) _____

(expression of encouragement)

(1) _____

(expression of confusion)

(1) _____

(expression of doubt)

(1) _____

(expression of disgust)

(1) _____

(expression of embarrassment)

(1) _____

(expression of affection)

(1) _____

(expression of pleasure)

(1) _____

(expression of concern)

When you revise your friendly letter, use these expressions to strengthen your writing voice. By adding a few of these expressions, you can make your writing sound more natural — as if you are talking directly to your friend.

Name _____

Drama on the High Seas

Complete each sentence below by writing a vocabulary word from the box.

1. Those opposing slavery were called <u>abolitionists</u> **(1 point)** .

2. A group whose views are respected by leaders is considered to be <u>influential</u> **(1)** .

3. If you have helped a person, you have <u>assisted</u> **(1)** him or her.

4. An argument is one type of <u>conflict</u> **(1)** .

5. Changing direction while sailing is <u>tacking</u> **(1)** .

6. If you have told a group that their plan seems solid, you have <u>encouraged</u> **(1)** them to carry it out.

7. Another word for *prisoners* is <u>captives</u> **(1)** .

8. If you feel strong fear, you feel <u>dread</u> **(1)** .

9. <u>Enslavement</u> **(1)** is preventing people from living in freedom.

10. A <u>privateer</u> **(1)** was a private ship given papers by a government allowing it to attack ships of another country.

11. A person learning a trade is an <u>apprentice</u> **(1)** .

Choose one of the vocabulary words and write a sentence.

(1) _____

_____

James Forten and the Revolutionary War

Complete the chart as you read the selection.

What I Know	What I Want to Know	What I Learned
Answers will vary.	Answers will vary.	**(2 points each)**
Samples provided.	Samples provided.	
James Forten was an	What was James	
African American boy.	Forten's job on the ship?	
He served on a ship	Did he fight in any	
during the American	battles?	
Revolution.	What did he do after the	
	war?	

Name _____

Did It Really Happen?

The sentences below tell about James Forten. Write T if the sentence is true, or F if the sentence is false. If a sentence is false, correct it to make it true.

1. __F (1)__ New York, where James Forten was born, was home to many significant abolitionists.

   Philadelphia, where James Forten was born, was home to many significant

   abolitionists.

2. __F (1)__ James became a foot soldier when he was 14 years old.

   His mother finally let him become a sailor when he was 14 years old.

   _____

3. __T (1)__ On his second voyage, James Forten and the crew of the *Royal Louis* were

   captured and held captive on board the British prison ship *Jersey*.

   _____

   _____

4. __F (1)__ James feared he would be killed by the British.

   James feared he would be sold into slavery by the British.

   _____

5. __T (1)__ It was probably George Washington's victory over the British

   that saved Forten.

   _____

   _____

6. __F (1)__ After the war, James Forten became a wealthy politician and

   an influential abolitionist.

   After the war, James Forten became a wealthy sailmaker and an influential

   abolitionist.

Assessment Tip: Total **6** Points

Name _____

Step by Step

Read the directions. Then answer the questions on page 234.

"Wild Snake" Marble Game

This marble game provides good marble-shooting practice.

Players: Two or more

Materials: One marble per player; a stick or a piece of chalk

Object: The winner is the last player left in the game.

How to Play:

1. If the game is played on sand, scratch seven circles to form a course. If it is played on cement, draw seven circles with chalk. The course may go in any direction.

2. Make a starting line and place all players' marbles behind it.

3. Taking turns, players try to land their marble in the first circle by flicking it with their thumb or finger.

4. A player who lands a marble in the first circle proceeds to the second one, and so on.

5. A player who gets to the seventh circle must complete the course in reverse.

6. Players who complete the course forward and backward are "wild snakes." This means that they may shoot at the other players' marbles.

7. If a player's marble is hit by the marble of a wild snake, that player is out of the game (even if that player is also a wild snake).

8. If a wild snake's marble lands in a circle while trying to shoot another player's marble, the wild snake is out of the game.

Name _____

Step by Step   continued

Answer these questions about the directions on page 233.

1. What do the directions teach readers?

   how to play a marble game called "Wild Snake" **(2 points)**

   _____

2. In order to follow these directions, what should you do first?

   Read the directions all the way through. **(2)**

   _____

3. What does each player need before play can begin?

   a marble **(2)**

   _____

4. Why do you need chalk if you are playing the game on cement?

   You need to draw seven circles on the cement. **(2)**

   _____

5. How does a player become a "wild snake"?

   The player moves through the course, first forward, then in

   reverse, by flicking a marble into each circle. **(2)**

6. What can cause a wild snake to be out of the game?

   being hit by another wild snake's marble; landing in a circle **(2)**

   _____

7. What would happen if you did step number two before doing step
   number one?

   The marbles would be lined up, but there would be no course to

   follow. **(2)**

Assessment Tip: Total **14** Points

Name _____

Prefix Plus

Use the charts to figure out the meaning of each underlined word.
Then rewrite the word in the blank space, using the clues. The first
one has been done for you. Sample answers shown.

Prefix	Meaning
sub-	under, below
sur-	over, above

Word Root	Meaning
mit	to cause to go
ject	to throw
vey	to look
merge	to plunge

Base Words
mount (climb)
standard (usual quality)
face (part)
pass

1. The rebels would not <u>submit</u> to unfair British laws.

   The rebels would not ____go under____ unfair British laws.

2. The naval officer <u>surveyed</u> the harbor.

   The naval officer ___looked over **(2)**___ the harbor.

3. A harbor seal <u>submerged</u> near the ship.

   A harbor seal ___plunged under **(2)**___ near the ship.

4. Soon, the seal came to the <u>surface</u> of the ocean.

   Soon, the seal came to the ___above part **(2)**___ of the ocean.

5. The prisoners were <u>subjected</u> to punishment.

   The prisoners were ___thrown under **(2)**___ punishment.

6. James thought the tattered sailcloth was <u>substandard</u>.

   James thought the tattered sailcloth was ___below the usual quality **(2)**___.

7. With his positive attitude, James could <u>surmount</u> any problem.

   James could ___climb over **(2)**___ any problem.

8. James's sails <u>surpassed</u> any others.

   James's sails ___passed above **(2)**___ any others.

Name _____

Final /l/ or /əl/

The final /l/ or /əl/ sounds are usually spelled with two letters.
When you hear these sounds, think of the patterns *le*, *el*, and *al*.

/l/ or /əl/   spar**le**, jew**el**, leg**al**

► The spellings of *fossil* and *devil* differ from the usual spelling
patterns. The /əl/ sounds in these words are spelled *il*.

Write each Spelling Word under its spelling of the final /l/ or
/əl/ sound. Order of answers for each category may vary.

1. jewel
2. sparkle
3. angle
4. shovel
5. single
6. normal
7. angel
8. legal
9. whistle
10. fossil*
11. puzzle
12. bushel
13. mortal
14. gentle
15. level
16. label
17. pedal
18. ankle
19. needle
20. devil*

le

sparkle **(1 point)**

angle **(1)**

single **(1)**

whistle **(1)**

puzzle **(1)**

gentle **(1)**

ankle **(1)**

needle **(1)**

el

jewel **(1)**

shovel **(1)**

angel **(1)**

bushel **(1)**

level **(1)**

label **(1)**

al

normal **(1)**

legal **(1)**

mortal **(1)**

pedal **(1)**

Another Spelling

fossil **(1)**

devil **(1)**

Assessment Tip: Total **20** Points

Name _____

Spelling Spree

Ending Match For each beginning syllable, choose the correct spelling of the /l/ or /əl/ sound to form a Spelling Word. Then write each word correctly.

1. spar-   -kel   (-kle)   -kal   1. sparkle **(1)**
2. gen-   (-tle)   -tal   -til   2. gentle **(1)**
3. fos-   -sle   -sal   (-sil)   3. fossil **(1)**
4. puz-   -zel   (-zle)   -el   4. puzzle **(1)**
5. la-   (-bel)   -bal   -ble   5. label **(1)**
6. whis-   -tel   (-tle)   -tal   6. whistle **(1)**
7. mor-   -tle   -tel   (-tal)   7. mortal **(1)**

Crack the Code Some Spelling Words have been written in the following code. Use the code to figure out each word. Then write each word correctly.

CODE:	R	E	N	O	T	V	A	G	B	F	Y	M
LETTER:	A	D	E	G	I	J	K	L	N	P	V	W

8. RBAGN   ankle **(1)**
9. GNYNG   level **(1)**
10. RBONG   angel **(1)**
11. BNNEGN   needle **(1)**
12. RBOGN   angle **(1)**
13. VNMNG   jewel **(1)**
14. ENYTG   devil **(1)**
15. FNERG   pedal **(1)**

Spelling Words

1. jewel
2. sparkle
3. angle
4. shovel
5. single
6. normal
7. angel
8. legal
9. whistle
10. fossil*
11. puzzle
12. bushel
13. mortal
14. gentle
15. level
16. label
17. pedal
18. ankle
19. needle
20. devil*

Theme 3: **Voices of the Revolution**   237

Assessment Tip: Total **15** Points

Name _____

Proofreading and Writing

Proofreading Circle the five misspelled Spelling Words in the following **Help Wanted** advertisement. Then write each word correctly.

Spelling Words

> **Are you tired** of doing dirty work with a (shovle?) Maybe you're sick of hauling (bushal) baskets of vegetables to market. We're looking for a hard-working, (singel) young man or woman to be an apprentice in the sailmaking business. You must be of (legil) working age, and you should be willing to work with a large needle.
>
> **Please apply in person during (normel) business hours at the office of James Forten, Sailmaker.**

Spelling Words

1. jewel
2. sparkle
3. angle
4. shovel
5. single
6. normal
7. angel
8. legal
9. whistle
10. fossil*
11. puzzle
12. bushel
13. mortal
14. gentle
15. level
16. label
17. pedal
18. ankle
19. needle
20. devil*

1. shovel **(1 point)**
2. bushel **(1)**
3. single **(1)**
4. legal **(1)**
5. normal **(1)**

━━━ **Write a Character Sketch** James Forten had an unusual life. At various times he was a sailor in the Revolutionary War, a sailmaker, a successful businessman, and an abolitionist. Is there anything about his personality that you think would have helped him in the different parts of his life?

On a separate sheet of paper, write a brief character sketch of James Forten. Use Spelling Words from the list.
Responses will vary. **(5)**

Assessment Tip: Total **10** Points

Name _____

Journal of Opposites

Read the journal. In each blank, write an antonym of the clue word.
Sample answers shown.

December 31, 1781

This summer I set sail aboard the *Royal Louis*. We were ready to

fight the ___powerful **(1 point)**___ British navy. Soon we were caught up
(powerless)

in battle with the ___heavily **(1)**___ armed ship *Active*. I carried
(lightly)

gunpowder from ___below **(1)**___ the decks to the guns. In time,
(above)

the *Active* surrendered by ___lowering **(1)**___ its flag. I'll never
(raising)

forget the crowd's excited ___cheering **(1)**___ as we took the ship
(booing)

back to Philadelphia. But our next trip out was ___unlucky **(1)**___.
(lucky)

Our ship surrendered to three British ships, and we crew members were

___captured **(1)**___ as prisoners. At least the boys were
(set free)

___allowed **(1)**___ to play marbles. The captain's son joined us,
(forbidden)

and we became ___friends **(1)**___. I wonder if this friendship
(enemies)

saved me from being ___sold **(1)**___ into slavery.
(bought)

Name _____

What Kind? How Many? Which One?

Adjectives A word that describes a noun or a pronoun is called an **adjective**. It tells what kind or how many. *A*, *an*, and *the* are special adjectives called **articles**. *A* and *an* refer to any item. *The* refers to a particular item. *This*, *that*, *these*, and *those* are **demonstrative adjectives**. They tell which one. *This* and *these* refer to nearby items; *that* and *those* refer to farther away items.

Circle all of the adjectives in the following sentences, including articles and demonstrative adjectives.

1. James sewed (straight) seams on (large), (square) sails. **(3 points)**
2. (Those) ships needed (many) sails. **(2)**
3. (Six) sailors are pulling on (the) (thick) ropes. **(3)**
4. (This) (huge) vessel is (impressive.) **(3)**
5. (Tired) merchants closed (the) shops. **(2)**
6. (Grateful) citizens will raise (a) cheer for (these) sailors. **(3)**
7. (An) anchor is thrown overboard. **(1)**
8. (A) (white) seagull dives for (the) (slippery) fish. **(4)**
9. (That) shop sells sails and (other) equipment for ships. **(2)**
10. Philadelphia has (a) (proud) heritage. **(2)**

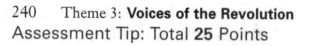

240   Theme 3: **Voices of the Revolution**
Assessment Tip: Total **25** Points

Name _____

Who Settled Where?

Proper Adjectives A **proper adjective** is formed from a proper noun and always begins with a capital letter.

Fill in the blank with the proper adjective formed from the proper noun in parentheses. Check a dictionary if you need to. (Number four is tricky!)

1. The state of Louisiana was once a <u>French **(1)**</u>_____ colony. (France)

2. The <u>American **(1)**</u>_____ Revolution was a fight for independence from England. (America)

3. King George III sat on the <u>English **(1)**</u>_____ throne. (England)

4. There were <u>Dutch **(1)**</u>_____ settlers in New York. (Holland)

5. <u>Spanish **(1)**</u>_____ explorers settled parts of Florida. (Spain)

6. Margaret's <u>German **(1)**</u>_____ ancestors settled in Pennsylvania. (Germany)

7. Many <u>Irish **(1)**</u>_____ immigrants came to America in the nineteenth century. (Ireland)

8. James Forten's ancestors were <u>African **(1)**</u>_____. (Africa)

9. Alaska was once a <u>Russian **(1)**</u>_____ territory. (Russia)

10. General Washington fought <u>British **(1)**</u>_____ soldiers. (Britain)

Name _____

Marvelous Marbles

Expanding Sentences with Adjectives Good writers add interest to
their writing by adding adjectives that help readers visualize a scene.

**Add adjectives to the following sentences to make them more lively
and interesting. Use your imagination!** Answers will vary.

1. These __**(1 point)**_____ children are playing with
   marbles.

2. That __**(1)**_____ bag holds __**(1)**_____
   marbles.

3. Alfred sits on the __**(1)**_____ ground to play.

4. Carla shows Tony a __**(1)**_____ marble.

5. The players enjoy the __**(1)**_____ sunshine.

6. Kinley doesn't play marbles, but he collects __**(1)**_____
   cards.

7. That __**(1)**_____ girl usually wins.

8. The __**(1)**_____ boy in the __**(1)**_____
   jacket won today!

Assessment Tip: Total **10** Points

Name _____

Writing a Biography

In *James Forten*, you read about an African American sailor who served during the Revolutionary War. A **biography** is a written account of important events and significant experiences in a person's life. Before you write a biography of your own, follow these steps:

► Choose a real person whom you admire or a person who lived during the American Revolution.

► Research important facts, dates, places, events, and accomplishments in this person's life. Use the Internet, reference books, or history books in your library to gather information.

Record and organize important dates, locations, and events in this person's life on the timeline below. (2 points each)

The Life of _____

DATE	EVENT
_____	
_____	
_____	
_____	
_____	

Now write your biography on a separate sheet of paper. Start with an anecdote or a famous quotation from this person's life. Then work from your timeline. Write about important events and experiences, using chronological order, time-order words, and key dates. Highlight the events that you think best reveal this person's character or major accomplishments. Finally, conclude by summarizing why this person is remembered. (5)

Name _____

Capitalizing Names of People and Places

Good biographers proofread their writing to check for correct
capitalization of proper names. Imagine you have written a biography
of James Forten. The book jacket will include information to interest
readers in the book.

**Proofread the following book-jacket sentences. Underline the
names of people and places that should be capitalized and write
them correctly on the lines. (1 point each)**

African American sailor <u>james forten</u> was born in <u>philadelphia</u> in 1766.

James Forten, Philadelphia

Living on the shores of the <u>atlantic ocean</u>, he dreamed of glory on the
high seas.

Atlantic Ocean

When he was only fourteen years old, he joined the crew of a vessel that
was commanded by <u>captain stephen decatur</u>.

Captain Stephen Decatur

The *royal louis* was a privateer, or a privately owned ship that the <u>united
states</u> used in the war against <u>england</u>.

Royal Louis, United States, England

After the British captured his ship in 1781, the teenaged sailor was
imprisoned in the filthy hold of a prison ship, the *jersey*, which was
anchored off <u>new york</u>.

Jersey, New York

This young patriot feared little — except the bitter chance that he would
be sent to the <u>west indies</u> and enslaved.

West Indies

Name _____

Code Words

Use the words in the box to complete the sentences below.

Vocabulary

retreats   intend   courier   timid   suspect

**Write the words next to their definitions. Unscramble the circled
letters to answer the question that follows.**

1. to mistrust s u s p (e) c t **(2 points)**

2. to plan to do something i n t e n (d) to do **(2)**

3. person who delivers messages (c) (o) u r i e r **(2)**

4. shy or frightened t i m i (d) **(2)**

5. times when an army runs away from an attack
   r e t r (e) a t s **(2)**

What do you do to a secret message to read it?

d e c o d e **(2 points)**

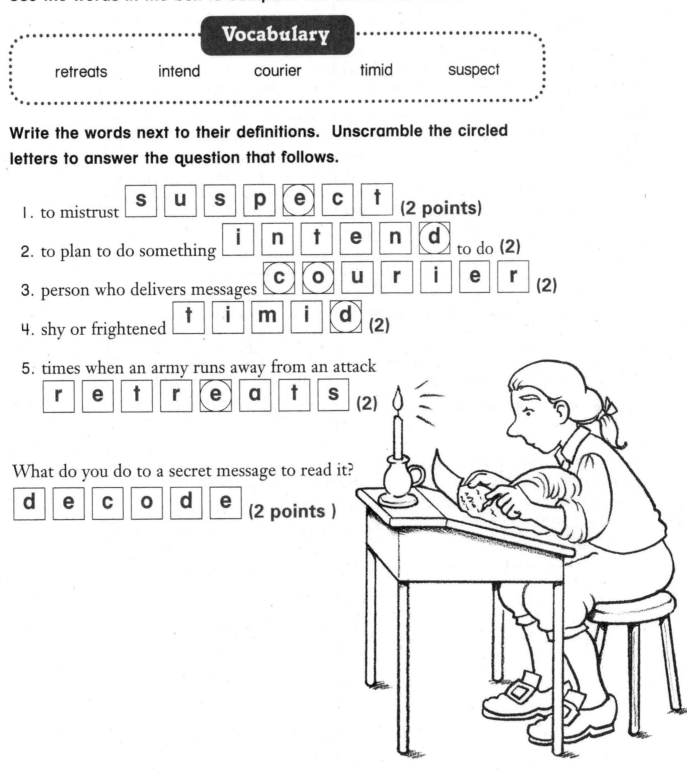

Name _____

Effective Spies

After reading each selection, complete the chart below to show what you learned. Wording of answers will vary.

Toliver's Secret	
Cause	**Effect**
Ellen's grandfather has hurt his ankle.	He can't deliver the message for General Washington, so he asks Ellen to do it for him. **(3 points)**
Ellen dresses in her brother's old clothes and cuts off her hair. **(3)**	Ellen looks like a boy.

Mary Redmond, John Darragh, and Dicey Langston: Spies	
Cause	**Effect**
Mary Redmond sees two British soldiers eyeing her partner.	She tackles her partner, and takes the secret message from his jacket. **(3)**
John's mother hides the messages inside large cloth-covered buttons on John's coat. **(3)**	The British soldiers at the checkpoint do not find the messages John Darragh is carrying.

Assessment Tip: Total **12** Points

Name _____

Mood Chart

Use the chart below to compare and contrast the moods in *Toliver's Secret* and *And Then What Happened, Paul Revere?*

Sample answers are given. Accept reasonable responses.

Toliver's Secret

Page 334B: *And then the British army came to New York and there had been three months of defeat. "If you understand how important it is to take the message, Ellen, I'll tell you how it can be done. And then you are to decide." Ellen listened and didn't say a word.*	Mood Created: **(1 point)** Sample answers: serious, dangerous Key Words and Phrases: Sample answers: months of defeat; important; didn't say a word **(1)**
Page 334F: *She ran into the shop to show her grandfather how she looked. For the first time since he fell on the ice, Grandfather laughed. "You look like a ragged little urchin all right," he said, "with those holes in your elbows. But all the better. No one will even notice you."*	Mood Created: Sample answers: cheerful, hopeful **(1)** Key Words and Phrases: Sample answers: ran into the shop; laughed; all the better **(1)**

And Then What Happened, Paul Revere?

Page 269: *From Boston to Cambridge to Watertown to Worcester to Hartford (Watch out, dogs on the road! Watch out, chickens!) to New York to Philadelphia he went. And back. 63 miles a day. (This was not swatting flies!)*	Mood Created: Sample answers: silly; wild **(1)** Key Words and Phrases: Sample answers: Watch out, chickens!; This was not swatting flies! **(1)**
Page 273: *And then suddenly from out of the shadows appeared six English officers. They rode up with their pistols in their hands and ordered Paul to stop. But Paul didn't stop immediately. "Stop!" one of the officers shouted. "If you go an inch farther, you are a dead man."*	Mood Created: Sample answers: dangerous; exciting **(1)** Key Words and Phrases: Sample answers: suddenly; out of the shadows; pistols; you are a dead man **(1)**

Assessment Tip: Total **8** Points

Name _____

Vocabulary Match

For each item, circle the letter of the answer that best fits the underlined vocabulary word.

1. The spy searched the market and tried to spot his <u>contacts</u>.
   A. friends
   B. connections **(2 points)**
   C. students
   D. soldiers

2. The woman tried to look <u>casual</u> as she handed off the secret message.
   A. happy
   B. not concerned **(2)**
   C. sad
   D. dangerous

3. The message was <u>encoded</u> so that the British would not be able to read it.
   A. unclear
   B. listened to
   C. written with secret symbols **(2)**
   D. read aloud

4. The spy secretly stuffed the message in his shoe, knowing he would be in great <u>peril</u> if anyone saw him.
   A. water
   B. safety
   C. danger **(2)**
   D. confusion

5. Now he had to cross a river full of British boats, and he <u>steeled</u> himself for this terrifying trip.
   A. doubted
   B. talked to
   C. strengthened **(2)**
   D. weakened

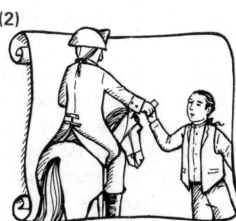

Assessment Tip: Total **10** Points

Name _____

Test Practice

Use the three steps you've learned to write a personal response to these questions about *Mary Redmond, John Darragh, and Dicey Langston: Spies*. Make a chart on a separate paper. Then write your response on the lines below.

1. Would you have done what Mary, John, or Dicey did? Explain why you would or would not risk your life as they did.

Use the Personal Response Checklist to score each student's response.

_____

_____

_____

_____

_____

_____

_____

_____

_____

_____

_____

_____

Personal Response Checklist

✔ Did I restate the question at the beginning? **(2 points)**

✔ Can I add more details from what I read to support my answer? **(5)**

✔ Can I add more of my thoughts or experiences to support my answer? **(5)**

✔ Do I need to delete any details that do not help answer the question? **(2)**

✔ Where can I add more exact words? **(2)**

✔ Did I use clear handwriting? Did I make any mistakes? **(4)**

Continue on page 250.

Test Practice continued

2. Connecting/Comparing Both Dicey Langston and James Forten show courage. Besides courage, what qualities do you most admire in both Dicey and James? Why do you admire these qualities?

Use the Personal Response Checklist to score each student's response.

_____

_____

_____

_____

_____

_____

_____

_____

_____

_____

_____

_____

_____

Personal Response Checklist

✔ Did I restate the question at the beginning? **(2 points)**

✔ Can I add more details from what I read to support my answer? **(5)**

✔ Can I add more of my thoughts or experiences to support my answer? **(5)**

✔ Do I need to delete any details that do not help answer the question? **(2)**

✔ Where can I add more exact words? **(2)**

✔ Did I use clear handwriting? Did I make any mistakes? **(4)**

Read your answers to Questions 1 and 2 aloud to a partner. Then discuss the questions on the checklist. Make any changes that will improve your answers.

Assessment Tip: Total **40** Points

Name _____

Author's Viewpoint

Read the paragraph below. Then answer the questions.

George Washington was a most remarkable man. He is truly worthy of the title "Father of the Country." First, Washington led the army that defeated the British during the Revolutionary War. He then served as a leader of the effort to write the United States Constitution. As if that weren't enough, he went on to serve as the new country's first President.

1. What is the author's viewpoint of George Washington?

   Sample answer: The author greatly admires Washington. **(2 points)**

2. What words reveal the author's opinions about Washington?

   a most remarkable man; truly worthy of the title; as if that wasn't enough **(3)**

3. What facts does the author include in support of his or her viewpoint?

   Washington led the army that defeated the British. **(1)**

   He led the effort to write the United States Constitution. **(1)**

   He was the new country's first President. **(1)**

Name _____

Follow the Steps

Read the directions. Then answer the questions below.

How to Carry a Secret Message
What You'll Need: pen or pencil, sheet of paper, large loaf of unsliced bread, bread knife, handkerchief

Steps:

1. Write your secret message on the paper.
2. Fold the paper into a small square or rectangle. It should be half the width of the loaf of bread.
3. Carefully cut a rectangle in the bottom of the loaf of bread. Make sure the slice you cut doesn't break.
4. Place the message inside the space in the loaf.
5. Put the slice back into the space.
6. Wrap the loaf in a handkerchief so that the message is on the bottom.

Now you are ready to deliver your message.

(Wording of answers may vary. Sample responses shown.)

1. What do the directions show how to do?
   how to carry a secret message **(2 points)**
   _____

2. To follow these directions correctly, what is the first thing you should do?
   Read the directions from beginning to end. **(2)**
   _____

3. What materials do you need to gather before you begin?
   a pen or pencil, sheet of paper, loaf of bread, bread knife, handkerchief **(2)**
   _____

4. Why do you have to make sure that the slice of bread you cut doesn't break?
   because you will use it to cover up the space you have made **(2)**
   _____

5. What would happen if you did Step 5 before Step 4?
   The message wouldn't be hidden inside the loaf of bread. **(2)**
   _____

Assessment Tip: Total **10** Points

Match Words and Meanings

Read the sentences. Then read the definitions. Draw a line from each sentence to the definition that goes with the underlined word.
(**1 point** for each correct match)

1. Will the climbers <u>surmount</u> the peak before nightfall?

2. The <u>submarine</u> dove deep beneath the surface.

3. We should explore the tide pools only after the big waves <u>subside</u>.

4. They hope to <u>surpass</u> the current record very soon.

5. Riding the <u>subway</u> is the fastest way to get downtown.

6. Any <u>surplus</u> canned food can be donated to the shelter.

7. The <u>surcharge</u> on each ticket is $1.75.

8. They plan to <u>subdivide</u> the land into four smaller plots.

a. "sink down to a lower level"

b. "amount beyond what is needed"

c. "added amount that must be paid"

d. "a ship that goes underwater"

e. "make into smaller pieces"

f. "a train that travels underground"

g. "go to the top of"

h. "go beyond"

Antonym Crossword

Read the words in the box. Then read the crossword puzzle clues.
Complete the puzzle by writing the correct antonym for each clue.

(1 point each)

Word Bank

backward	fiction	melt	public
deep	forget	plain	start
difficult	laugh	problem	wild

Across

1. easy
4. cry
6. fancy
7. tame
9. solution
11. finish

Down

1. shallow
2. fact
3. private
5. forward
8. remember
10. freeze

Assessment Tip: Total **12** Points

Name _____

Spelling Review

Write Spelling Words from the list on this page to answer the questions. Order of answers in each category may vary.

1–12. Which twelve words have the final /ər/ sounds?

1. polar **(1 point)**

2. humor **(1)**

3. mayor **(1)**

4. lunar **(1)**

5. tractor **(1)**

6. quarter **(1)**

7. parlor **(1)**

8. powder **(1)**

9. actor **(1)**

10. matter **(1)**

11. shoulder **(1)**

12. burglar **(1)**

13–23. Which eleven words have the final /l/ or /əl/ sounds?

13. jewel **(1)**

14. needle **(1)**

15. legal **(1)**

16. gentle **(1)**

17. equal **(1)**

18. mortal **(1)**

19. sparkle **(1)**

20. bushel **(1)**

21. single **(1)**

22. whistle **(1)**

23. pedal **(1)**

24–30. What syllable is missing from each word? Write each word.

24. sor— sorrow **(1)**

25. —have behave **(1)**

26. wed— wedding **(1)**

27. rap— rapid **(1)**

28. —ware aware **(1)**

29. —ue value **(1)**

30. pub— publish **(1)**

Spelling Words

1. jewel
2. polar
3. needle
4. humor
5. legal
6. mayor
7. gentle
8. lunar
9. sorrow
10. tractor
11. quarter
12. behave
13. parlor
14. wedding
15. powder
16. actor
17. rapid
18. equal
19. mortal
20. aware
21. matter
22. sparkle
23. shoulder
24. bushel
25. value
26. publish
27. single
28. whistle
29. burglar
30. pedal

Name _____

Spelling Spree

Syllable Rhymes Write the Spelling Word that has a first
syllable that rhymes with each word below.

1. win   single **(1 point)**

2. car   sparkle **(1)**

3. rub   publish **(1)**

4. push   bushel **(1)**

5. fur   burglar **(1)**

6. den   gentle **(1)**

7. map   rapid **(1)**

Spelling Words

1. humor
2. gentle
3. lunar
4. tractor
5. quarter
6. rapid
7. mortal
8. sparkle
9. bushel
10. publish
11. single
12. burglar
13. pedal
14. jewel
15. mayor

Word Fun Write a Spelling Word to fit each clue.

8. Change the last three letters in *jelly* to make a word meaning
"gem." jewel **(1)**

9. Change the first three letters of *final* to make a word
describing what you do to make a bicycle move. pedal **(1)**

10. Add a consonant to *moral* to make a word meaning "human
being." mortal **(1)**

11. Change the word *quartz* to make it mean "twenty-five cents." quarter **(1)**

12. Remove two letters from *detractor* to form a word for a farm machine.
tractor **(1)**

13. Replace two consonants in *lunch* to form a word having to do with
the moon. lunar **(1)**

14. Replace two letters in *humid* to make a word that tells what makes
people laugh. humor **(1)**

15. Change one letter in *major* to make the head of a city. mayor **(1)**

Assessment Tip: Total **15** Points

Name _____

Proofreading and Writing

Proofreading Circle the five misspelled Spelling Words in
this report. Then write each word correctly.

Betsy Ross sat in her (parler) with a few scraps of cloth, a
(needel) and some thread. She usually made jackets, (weding)
dresses, and lacy shirts. That day, she made a flag with great
(valyew) for the new nation. It made the colonial army (equel) to
the British.

1. powder
2. polar
3. matter
4. parlor
5. equal
6. aware
7. behave
8. sorrow
9. shoulder
10. value
11. whistle
12. needle
13. legal
14. actor
15. wedding

1. parlor **(1 point)** _____
2. needle **(1)** _____
3. wedding **(1)** _____
4. value **(1)** _____
5. equal **(1)** _____

Title Trouble Correct the following book titles. Replace each
underlined word with a rhyming Spelling Word.

6. *Soldiers, Keep Your Chowder Close By* Powder **(1)** _____

7. *Just Thistle, I'll Come Running!* Whistle **(1)** _____

8. *The Factor Who Makes History Come Alive* Actor **(1)** _____

9. *One Soldier's Borrow; Another's Joy* Sorrow **(1)** _____

10. *Be Compare of Danger Signs* Aware **(1)** _____

11. *Manners: How a Soldier Should Shave* Behave **(1)** _____

12. *Valley Forge—Cold as Solar Ice* Polar **(1)** _____

13. *He Carried His Musket on His Boulder* Shoulder **(1)** _____

14. *The New Flag Really Does Flatter!* Matter **(1)** _____

15. *The Regal Papers* Legal **(1)** _____

✏ **Write a Diary Entry** On a separate sheet of paper, write a
diary entry telling about a colonial American's day. Use the Spelling
Review Words. Responses will vary. **(5 points)**

Name _____

Making Verbs Agree
with Subjects

**Complete each sentence with a present tense form of the verb in
parentheses. Be sure it agrees with the subject in number.**

1. The girl ___has **(1 point)**___ a short haircut. (have)

2. Her cap ___is **(1)**___ red with white stripes. (be)

3. Mittens ___keep **(1)**___ her hands warm. (keep)

4. Warm corncakes ___smell **(1)**___ delicious. (smell)

5. Her grandfather ___has **(1)**___ given her a hidden message. (have)

6. A messenger ___risks **(1)**___ severe punishment. (risk)

7. The local boatmen ___are **(1)**___ kindly. (be)

8. Friends ___await **(1)**___ the girl at a tavern. (await)

9. Coins ___jingle **(1)**___ in the girl's pocket. (jingle)

10. The girl ___takes **(1)**___ a deep breath. (take)

Assessment Tip: Total **10** Points

Name _____

Writing Past Tense Verbs

Complete each sentence. Use the past tense form of the verb in parentheses. You may need to check irregular verbs in your dictionary.

1. A farmer _____rowed **(1 point)**_____ his boat across the water. (row)

2. He _____tied **(1)**_____ a rope from the boat to the dock. (tie)

3. He _____met **(1)**_____ a Patriot near the marketplace. (meet)

4. The Patriot _____gave **(1)**_____ the farmer a packet. (give)

5. The farmer _____hid **(1)**_____ the packet in the lining of his coat. (hide)

6. The farmer _____squeezed **(1)**_____ the Patriot's hand. (squeeze)

7. He _____brought **(1)**_____ a basket of vegetables to the marketplace. (bring)

8. The farmer _____sold **(1)**_____ the vegetables to a friend. (sell)

9. They _____talked **(1)**_____ about the progress of the Revolution. (talk)

10. Then he _____returned **(1)**_____ to his boat with the hidden message. (return)

Student Handbook

Contents

How to Study a Word

1. LOOK at the word.
  ▸ What does the word mean?
  ▸ What letters are in the word?
  ▸ Name and touch each letter.

2. SAY the word.
  ▸ Listen for the consonant sounds.
  ▸ Listen for the vowel sounds.

3. THINK about the word.
  ▸ How is each sound spelled?
  ▸ Close your eyes and picture the word.
  ▸ What familiar spelling patterns do you see?
  ▸ Did you see any prefixes, suffixes, or other word parts?

4. WRITE the word.
  ▸ Think about the sounds and the letters.
  ▸ Form the letters correctly.

5. CHECK the spelling.
  ▸ Did you spell the word the same way it is spelled in your word list?
  ▸ If you did not spell the word correctly, write the word again.

accept	buy	friend		
ache	by	goes		
again	calendar	going	ninth	tried
all right	cannot	grammar	often	tries
almost	can't	guard	once	truly
already	careful	guess	other	two
although	catch	guide	people	unknown
always	caught	half	principal	until
angel	chief	haven't	quiet	unusual
angle	children	hear	quit	wasn't
answer	choose	heard	quite	wear
argue	chose	heavy	really	weather
asked	color	height	receive	Wednesday
aunt	cough	here	rhythm	weird
author	cousin	hers	right	we'll
awful	decide	hole	Saturday	we're
babies	divide	hoping	stretch	weren't
been	does	hour	surely	we've
believe	don't	its	their	where
bother	early	it's	theirs	which
bought	enough	January	there	whole
break	every	let's	they're	witch
breakfast	exact	listen	they've	won't
breathe	except	loose	those	wouldn't
broken	excite	lose	though	write
brother	expect	minute	thought	writing
brought	February	muscle	through	written
bruise	finally	neighbor	tied	you're
build	forty	nickel	tired	yours
business	fourth	ninety	to	
busy	Friday	ninety-nine	too	

Take-Home Word List

Eye of the Storm

The /ā/, /ē/, and /ī/ Sounds

/ā/ ➡ m**a**le, cl**ai**m, str**ay**
/ē/ ➡ l**ea**f, fl**ee**t
/ī/ ➡ str**ike**, th**igh**, s**ign**

Spelling Words

1. speech
2. claim
3. strike
4. stray
5. fade
6. sign
7. leaf
8. thigh
9. thief
10. height
11. mild
12. waist
13. sway
14. beast
15. stain
16. fleet
17. stride
18. praise
19. slight
20. niece

Challenge Words

1. campaign
2. describe
3. cease
4. sacrifice
5. plight

My Study List
Add your own spelling words on the back. ➡

Take-Home Word List

Nature's Fury
Reading-Writing Workshop

Look for familiar spelling patterns in these words to help you remember their spellings.

Spelling Words

1. enough
2. caught
3. brought
4. thought
5. every
6. ninety
7. their
8. they're
9. there
10. there's
11. know
12. knew
13. o'clock
14. we're
15. people

Challenge Words

1. decent
2. stationery
3. stationary
4. correspond
5. reversible

My Study List
Add your own spelling words on the back. ➡

Take-Home Word List

Earthquake Terror

Short Vowels

/ă/ ➡ st**a**ff
/ĕ/ ➡ sl**e**pt
/ĭ/ ➡ m**i**st
/ŏ/ ➡ d**o**ck
/ŭ/ ➡ b**u**nk

Spelling Words

1. bunk
2. staff
3. dock
4. slept
5. mist
6. bunch
7. swift
8. stuck
9. breath
10. tough
11. fond
12. crush
13. grasp
14. dwell
15. fund
16. ditch
17. split
18. swept
19. deaf
20. rough

Challenge Words

1. trek
2. frantic
3. summit
4. rustic
5. mascot

My Study List
Add your own spelling words on the back. ➡

Name _____

My Study List

1. _____
2. _____
3. _____
4. _____
5. _____
6. _____
7. _____
8. _____
9. _____
10. _____

Review Words

1. trunk
2. skill
3. track
4. fresh
5. odd

How to Study a Word

Look at the word.
Say the word.
Think about the word.
Write the word.
Check the spelling.

266

Name _____

My Study List

1. _____
2. _____
3. _____
4. _____
5. _____
6. _____
7. _____
8. _____
9. _____
10. _____

How to Study a Word

Look at the word.
Say the word.
Think about the word.
Write the word.
Check the spelling.

266

Name _____

My Study List

1. _____
2. _____
3. _____
4. _____
5. _____
6. _____
7. _____
8. _____
9. _____
10. _____

Review Words

1. free
2. twice
3. gray
4. least
5. safe

How to Study a Word

Look at the word.
Say the word.
Think about the word.
Write the word.
Check the spelling.

266

Michelle Kwan: Heart of a Champion

Compound Words
wheel + chair =
  wheelchair
up + to + date =
  up-to-date
first + aid = first aid

Spelling Words

1. basketball
2. wheelchair
3. cheerleader
4. newscast
5. weekend
6. everybody
7. up-to-date
8. grandparent
9. first aid
10. wildlife
11. highway
12. daytime
13. whoever
14. test tube
15. turnpike
16. shipyard
17. homemade
18. household
19. salesperson
20. brother-in-law

Challenge Words

1. extraordinary
2. self-assured
3. quick-witted
4. limelight
5. junior high school

My Study List
Add your own spelling words on the back. ➡

Nature's Fury
Spelling Review

Spelling Words

1. slept
2. split
3. staff
4. fade
5. praise
6. slope
7. claim
8. stroll
9. mood
10. beast
11. crush
12. fond
13. dwell
14. strike
15. clue
16. boast
17. flute
18. sway
19. cruise
20. mild
21. grasp
22. swift
23. bunk
24. slight
25. thrown
26. stole
27. fleet
28. dew
29. youth
30. thigh

See the back for Challenge Words.

My Study List
Add your own spelling words on the back. ➡

Volcanoes

The /ō/, /o͞o/, and /yo͞o/ Sounds
/ō/ ➡ st**o**le, b**oa**st, thr**ow**n, str**o**ll
/o͞o/ or ➡ r**u**le, cl**ue**,
/yo͞o/   d**ew**, m**oo**d, cr**ui**se, r**ou**te

Spelling Words

1. thrown
2. stole
3. clue
4. dew
5. choose
6. rule
7. boast
8. cruise
9. stroll
10. route
11. mood
12. loaf
13. growth
14. youth
15. slope
16. bruise
17. loose
18. rude
19. flow
20. flute

Challenge Words

1. subdue
2. pursuit
3. molten
4. reproach
5. presume

My Study List
Add your own spelling words on the back. ➡

Name _____

My Study List

1. _____
2. _____
3. _____
4. _____
5. _____
6. _____
7. _____
8. _____
9. _____
10. _____

Review Words

1. group
2. goal
3. fruit
4. blew
5. broke

How to Study a Word

Look at the word.
Say the word.
Think about the word.
Write the word.
Check the spelling.

Name _____

My Study List

1. _____
2. _____
3. _____
4. _____
5. _____
6. _____
7. _____
8. _____
9. _____
10. _____

Challenge Words

1. frantic   6. rustic
2. trek   7. describe
3. cease   8. campaign
4. molten   9. subdue
5. pursuit   10. reproach

How to Study a Word

Look at the word.
Say the word.
Think about the word.
Write the word.
Check the spelling.

Name _____

My Study List

1. _____
2. _____
3. _____
4. _____
5. _____
6. _____
7. _____
8. _____
9. _____
10. _____

Review Words

1. afternoon
2. ninety-nine
3. everywhere
4. all right
5. breakfast

How to Study a Word

Look at the word.
Say the word.
Think about the word.
Write the word.
Check the spelling.

The Fear Place

The /ôr/, /âr/, and /är/ Sounds

/ôr/ ➡ torch, soar, sore

/âr/ ➡ hare, flair

/är/ ➡ scar

Spelling Words

1. hare
2. scar
3. torch
4. soar
5. harsh
6. sore
7. lord
8. flair
9. warn
10. floor
11. tore
12. lair
13. snare
14. carve
15. bore
16. fare
17. gorge
18. barge
19. flare
20. rare

Challenge Words

1. folklore
2. unicorn
3. ordinary
4. marvelous
5. hoard

My Study List
Add your own spelling words on the back. ➡

La Bamba

The /ou/, /ô/, and /oi/ Sounds

/ou/ ➡ ounce, tower

/ô/ ➡ claw, pause, bald

/oi/ ➡ moist, loyal

Spelling Words

1. hawk
2. claw
3. bald
4. tower
5. halt
6. prowl
7. loyal
8. pause
9. moist
10. ounce
11. launch
12. royal
13. scowl
14. haunt
15. noisy
16. coward
17. fawn
18. thousand
19. drown
20. fault

Challenge Words

1. announce
2. poise
3. loiter
4. somersault
5. awkward

My Study List
Add your own spelling words on the back. ➡

Give It All You've Got!
Reading-Writing Workshop

Look for familiar spelling patterns in these words to help you remember their spellings.

Spelling Words

1. would
2. wouldn't
3. clothes
4. happened
5. someone
6. sometimes
7. different
8. another
9. weird
10. eighth
11. coming
12. getting
13. going
14. stopped
15. here

Challenge Words

1. irresponsible
2. affectionate
3. brilliance
4. audible
5. menace

My Study List
Add your own spelling words on the back. ➡

Name _____

My Study List

1. _____
2. _____
3. _____
4. _____
5. _____
6. _____
7. _____
8. _____
9. _____
10. _____

How to Study a Word

Look at the word.
Say the word.
Think about the word.
Write the word.
Check the spelling.

Name _____

My Study List

1. _____
2. _____
3. _____
4. _____
5. _____
6. _____
7. _____
8. _____
9. _____
10. _____

Review Words

1. proud
2. dawn
3. false
4. cause
5. howl

How to Study a Word

Look at the word.
Say the word.
Think about the word.
Write the word.
Check the spelling.

Name _____

My Study List

1. _____
2. _____
3. _____
4. _____
5. _____
6. _____
7. _____
8. _____
9. _____
10. _____

Review Words

1. horse
2. sharp
3. square
4. stairs
5. board

How to Study a Word

Look at the word.
Say the word.
Think about the word.
Write the word.
Check the spelling.

And Then What Happened, Paul Revere?

Final /ər/

/ər/ → ang**er**, act**or**
pill**ar**

Spelling Words

1. theater
2. actor
3. mirror
4. powder
5. humor
6. anger
7. banner
8. pillar
9. major
10. thunder
11. flavor
12. finger
13. mayor
14. polar
15. clover
16. burglar
17. tractor
18. matter
19. lunar
20. quarter

Challenge Words

1. oyster
2. clamor
3. tremor
4. scholar
5. chamber

My Study List
Add your own spelling words on the back. ➡

Give It All You've Got! Spelling Review

Spelling Words

1. weekend
2. hawk
3. flair
4. stir
5. first aid
6. halt
7. royal
8. carve
9. worth
10. hurl
11. up-to-date
12. noisy
13. soar
14. barge
15. steer
16. wildlife
17. coward
18. gorge
19. return
20. smear
21. brother-in-law
22. thousand
23. tore
24. early
25. pearl
26. test tube
27. launch
28. snare
29. perch
30. wheelchair

See the back for Challenge Words.

My Study List
Add your own spelling words on the back. ➡

Mae Jemison

The /ûr/ and /îr/ Sounds

/ûr/ → g**er**m, st**ir**, ret**ur**n, **ear**ly, w**or**th

/îr/ → p**eer**, sm**ear**

Spelling Words

1. smear
2. germ
3. return
4. peer
5. stir
6. squirm
7. nerve
8. early
9. worth
10. pier
11. thirst
12. burnt
13. rear
14. term
15. steer
16. pearl
17. squirt
18. perch
19. hurl
20. worse

Challenge Words

1. interpret
2. yearn
3. emergency
4. dreary
5. career

My Study List
Add your own spelling words on the back. ➡

Name _____

My Study List

1. _____
2. _____
3. _____
4. _____
5. _____
6. _____
7. _____
8. _____
9. _____
10. _____

Review Words

1. learn
2. curve
3. world
4. firm
5. year

How to Study a Word

Look at the word.
Say the word.
Think about the word.
Write the word.
Check the spelling.

Name _____

My Study List

1. _____
2. _____
3. _____
4. _____
5. _____
6. _____
7. _____
8. _____
9. _____
10. _____

Challenge Words

1. extra-
   ordinary
2. announce
3. loiter
4. marvelous
5. yearn
6. self-assured
7. somersault
8. ordinary
9. emergency
10. dreary

How to Study a Word

Look at the word.
Say the word.
Think about the word.
Write the word.
Check the spelling.

Name _____

My Study List

1. _____
2. _____
3. _____
4. _____
5. _____
6. _____
7. _____
8. _____
9. _____
10. _____

Review Words

1. enter
2. honor
3. answer
4. collar
5. doctor

How to Study a Word

Look at the word.
Say the word.
Think about the word.
Write the word.
Check the spelling.

James Forten

Katie's Trunk

Voices of the Revolution
Reading-Writing Workshop

Final /l/ or /əl/

/l/ or
/əl/ ➡ sparkle,
jewel, legal

VCCV and VCV Patterns

VC|CV	VC|V	V|CV
ar|rive	val|ue	tu|lip
par|lor	clos|et	a|ware
		be|have

Look for familiar spelling patterns in these words to help you remember their spellings.

Spelling Words

1. jewel
2. sparkle
3. angle
4. shovel
5. single
6. normal
7. angel
8. legal
9. whistle
10. fossil
11. puzzle
12. bushel
13. mortal
14. gentle
15. level
16. label
17. pedal
18. ankle
19. needle
20. devil

Spelling Words

1. equal
2. parlor
3. collect
4. closet
5. perhaps
6. wedding
7. rapid
8. value
9. arrive
10. behave
11. shoulder
12. novel
13. tulip
14. sorrow
15. vanish
16. essay
17. publish
18. aware
19. subject
20. prefer

Spelling Words

1. happily
2. minute
3. beautiful
4. usually
5. instead
6. stretch
7. lying
8. excite
9. millimeter
10. divide
11. until
12. writing
13. tried
14. before
15. Saturday

Challenge Words

1. mineral
2. influential
3. vital
4. neutral
5. kernel

Challenge Words

1. device
2. skittish
3. logic
4. sincere
5. nuisance

Challenge Words

1. fatigue
2. antique
3. accumulate
4. camouflage
5. tongue

My Study List
Add your own spelling words on the back. ➡

My Study List
Add your own spelling words on the back. ➡

My Study List
Add your own spelling words on the back. ➡

Name _____

My Study List

1. _____
2. _____
3. _____
4. _____
5. _____
6. _____
7. _____
8. _____
9. _____
10. _____

How to Study a Word

Look at the word.
Say the word.
Think about the word.
Write the word.
Check the spelling.

274

Name _____

My Study List

1. _____
2. _____
3. _____
4. _____
5. _____
6. _____
7. _____
8. _____
9. _____
10. _____

Review Words

1. person
2. mistake
3. human
4. bottom
5. stomach

How to Study a Word

Look at the word.
Say the word.
Think about the word.
Write the word.
Check the spelling.

274

Name _____

My Study List

1. _____
2. _____
3. _____
4. _____
5. _____
6. _____
7. _____
8. _____
9. _____
10. _____

Review Words

1. simple
2. special
3. metal
4. nickel
5. double

How to Study a Word

Look at the word.
Say the word.
Think about the word.
Write the word.
Check the spelling.

274

Voices of the Revolution
Spelling Review

Spelling Words

1. powder	16. humor
2. burglar	17. behave
3. rapid	18. quarter
4. value	19. whistle
5. bushel	20. needle
6. actor	21. mayor
7. equal	22. sorrow
8. publish	23. parlor
9. tractor	24. mortal
10. pedal	25. gentle
11. polar	26. lunar
12. aware	27. shoulder
13. matter	28. jewel
14. single	29. legal
15. sparkle	30. wedding

See the back for Challenge Words.

My Study List
Add your own spelling words on the back. ➡

Name _____

My Study List

1. _____
2. _____
3. _____
4. _____
5. _____
6. _____
7. _____
8. _____
9. _____
10. _____

Challenge Words

1. oyster
2. skittish
3. influential
4. kernel
5. clamor
6. device
7. mineral
8. vital
9. sincere
10. scholar

How to Study a Word

Look at the word.
Say the word.
Think about the word.
Write the word.
Check the spelling.

Focus on Tall Tales

Vowel Changes: Long to Short
A long vowel sound may be spelled the same as a short vowel sound in words that are related in meaning.

Spelling Words

1.	steal	11.	crime
2.	stealth	12.	criminal
3.	cave	13.	breathe
4.	cavity	14.	breath
5.	wise	15.	wild
6.	wisdom	16.	wilderness
7.	deal	17.	shade
8.	dealt	18.	shadow
9.	athlete	19.	revise
10.	athletic	20.	revision

Challenge Words

1. volcano
2. volcanic
3. cycle
4. bicycle

My Study List
Add your own spelling words on the back. ➡

Focus on Poetry

Homophones
Homophones are words that sound the same but have different spellings and meanings.

Spelling Words

1.	cord	11.	role
2.	chord	12.	roll
3.	pray	13.	peel
4.	prey	14.	peal
5.	seam	15.	shone
6.	seem	16.	shown
7.	sole	17.	pain
8.	soul	18.	pane
9.	piece	19.	pole
10.	peace	20.	poll

Challenge Words

1. aisle
2. isle
3. rein
4. reign

My Study List
Add your own spelling words on the back. ➡

Name _____

My Study List

1. _____
2. _____
3. _____
4. _____
5. _____
6. _____
7. _____
8. _____
9. _____
10. _____

Review Words

1. final
2. finish
3. heal
4. health

How to Study a Word

Look at the word.
Say the word.
Think about the word.
Write the word.
Check the spelling.

Name _____

My Study List

1. _____
2. _____
3. _____
4. _____
5. _____
6. _____
7. _____
8. _____
9. _____
10. _____

Review Words

1. hall
2. haul
3. dear
4. deer

How to Study a Word

Look at the word.
Say the word.
Think about the word.
Write the word.
Check the spelling.

Problem Words

Words	Rules	Examples
bad badly	*Bad* is an adjective. It can be used after linking verbs like *look* and *feel*. *Badly* is an adverb.	This was a <u>bad</u> day. I feel <u>bad</u>. I play <u>badly</u>.
borrow lend	*Borrow* means "to take." *Lend* means "to give."	You may <u>borrow</u> my pen. I will <u>lend</u> it to you for the day.
can may	*Can* means "to be able to do something." *May* means "to be allowed or permitted."	Nellie <u>can</u> read quickly. May I borrow your book?
good well	*Good* is an adjective. *Well* is usually an adverb. It is an adjective only when it refers to health.	The weather looks <u>good</u>. She sings <u>well</u>. Do you feel <u>well</u>?
in into	*In* means "located within." *Into* means "movement from the outside to the inside."	Your lunch is <u>in</u> that bag. He jumped <u>into</u> the pool.
its it's	*Its* is a possessive pronoun. *It's* is a contraction of *it is*.	The dog wagged <u>its</u> tail. <u>It's</u> cold today.
let leave	*Let* means "to permit or allow." *Leave* means "to go away from" or "to let remain in place."	Please <u>let</u> me go swimming. I will <u>leave</u> soon. <u>Leave</u> it on my desk.
lie lay	*Lie* means "to rest or recline." *Lay* means "to put or place something."	The dog <u>lies</u> in its bed. Please <u>lay</u> the books there.

Problem Words continued

Words	Rules	Examples	
sit	*Sit* means "to rest in one place."	Please <u>sit</u> in this chair.	
set	*Set* means "to place or put."	<u>Set</u> the vase on the table.	
teach	*Teach* means "to give instruction."	He <u>teaches</u> us how to dance.	
learn	*Learn* means "to receive instruction."	I <u>learned</u> about history.	
their	*Their* is a possessive pronoun.	<u>Their</u> coats are on the bed.	
there	*There* is an adverb. It may also begin a sentence.	Is Carlos <u>there</u>? <u>There</u> is my book.	
they're	*They're* is a contraction of *they are*.	<u>They're</u> going to the store.	
two	*Two* is a number.	I bought <u>two</u> shirts.	
to	*To* means "in the direction of."	A squirrel ran <u>to</u> the tree.	
too	*Too* means "more than enough" and "also."	May we go <u>too</u>?	
whose	*Whose* is a possessive pronoun.	<u>Whose</u> tickets are these?	
who's	*Who's* is a contraction for *who is*.	<u>Who's</u> that woman?	
your	*Your* is a possessive pronoun.	Are these <u>your</u> glasses?	
you're	*You're* is a contraction for *you are*.	<u>You're</u> late again!	

Read each question below. Then check your paper. Correct any mistakes you find. After you have corrected them, put a check mark in the box next to the question.

☐ 1. Did I spell all the words correctly?

☐ 2. Did I indent each paragraph?

☐ 3. Does each sentence state a complete thought?

☐ 4. Are there any run-on sentences or fragments?

☐ 5. Did I begin each sentence with a capital letter?

☐ 6. Did I capitalize all proper nouns?

☐ 7. Did I end each sentence with the correct end mark?

☐ 8. Did I use commas, apostrophes, and quotation marks correctly?

Are there other problem areas you should watch for? Make your own proofreading checklist.

☐ _____

☐ _____

☐ _____

☐ _____

☐ _____

☐ _____

☐ _____

Proofreading Marks

Mark	Explanation	Examples
¶	Begin a new paragraph. Indent the paragraph.	¶The boat finally arrived. It was two hours late.
∧	Add letters, words, or sentences.	My ∧friend ate lunch with me t∧day. *best* *o*
ꝙ	Take out words, sentences, and punctuation marks. Correct spelling.	We looked at and admired, the moddel airplanes.
≡	Change a small letter to a capital letter.	New York city is exciting.
/	Change a capital letter to a small letter.	The Fireflies blinked in the dark.
⟨⟨ ⟩⟩	Add quotation marks.	⟨⟨Where do you want the piano?⟩⟩ asked the movers.
∧	Add a comma.	Carlton∧my cat∧has a mind of his own.
⊙	Add a period.	Put a period at the end of the sentence⊙
∾	Reverse letters or words.	Raed carefully the instructions.
?	Add a question mark.	Should I put the mark here ?
!	Add an exclamation mark.	Look out below !